THE "I LOVE MY AIR FRYER"

Baking

BOOK

From *Inside-Out Chocolate Chip Cookies* to
Calzones, 175 Quick and Easy Recipes

Robin Fields

Author of The "I Love My Air Fryer"
5-Ingredient Recipe Book

Adams Media

New York London Toronto Sydney New Delhi

Adams Media
An Imprint of Simon & Schuster, Inc.
100 Technology Center Drive
Stoughton, Massachusetts 02072

First Adams Media trade paperback edition September 2022

ADAMS MEDIA and colophon are trademarks of Simon & Schuster.

For information about special discounts for bulk purchases, please contact Simon & Schuster Special Sales at 1-866-506-1949 or business@simonandschuster.com.

The Simon & Schuster Speakers Bureau can bring authors to your live event. For more information or to book an event contact the Simon & Schuster Speakers Bureau at 1-866-248-3049 or visit our website at www.simonspeakers.com.

Interior layout by Michelle Kelly
Photographs by James Stefiuk

Manufactured in the United States of America

1 2022

Library of Congress Cataloging-in-Publication Data has been applied for.

ISBN 978-1-5072-1832-7
ISBN 978-1-5072-1833-4 (ebook)

Contains material adapted from the following title published by Adams Media, an Imprint of Simon & Schuster, Inc.: *The "I Love My Air Fryer" Keto Diet Recipe Book* by Sam Dillard, copyright © 2019, ISBN 978-1-5072-0992-9.

Contents

Introduction

Whether you're new to the air fryer or you've been using one for years, you know this appliance has revolutionized the kitchen. An air fryer can replace your microwave, deep fryer, and dehydrator, not to mention crisp up a basket of French fries...but did you know that it can also produce amazing baked goods in less time than your oven? That's right: If you can bake it, there's a good chance you can air fry it.

Air frying is so simple; if you can push a button or turn a dial, you already have all the skills you need to make delicious treats while saving time and energy. Air fryer baking is perfect if you have limited counter space, are traveling without access to a kitchen, or simply want to bring a new level of ease and convenience to baking.

No matter your motivation, you don't have to look any further than The "I Love My Air Fryer" Baking Book for all your baking needs. From savory goodies like Parmesan Garlic Knots and Spinach and Feta—Stuffed Bread to sweet indulgences like Chocolate Lava Cakes and Raspberry Lemon Bars, this book is your destination for breads, cakes, brownies, and other baked dishes your friends and family will love!

Along with 175 delicious recipes and dozens of mouthwatering photos, you'll also find kitchen hacks and flavoring suggestions to make baking in your air fryer even more convenient. From temperatures to cooking times, and handy bakeware tips, you'll discover tried-and-true tips in the chapters ahead. New to using an air fryer? Chapter 1 provides everything you need to know, from the different settings and functions to the additional tools you'll want to have on hand.

Throughout this book, you'll learn easy ways to create incredible baked goods in your new favorite kitchen appliance. Whether you're bringing a tray of cupcakes to a potluck or baking holiday cookies with your family, there are recipes for every occasion. So let's get baking with the air fryer!

Baking with an Air Fryer

Baking with an air fryer is as easy as using a microwave. Anybody can do it, and after just a few uses you'll wish you had switched over to this genius method of cooking earlier. This chapter will introduce you to air frying options and accessories to maximize your cooking time and get delicious, perfectly cooked results. It will also explain how to keep your air fryer clean and offer essentials you'll want to stock up on so that you can whip up delicious baked goods in no time!

While this chapter will cover the basics of air frying, the first step is reading the manual that came with your air fryer. The rise in popularity of the appliance means that you'll find a variety of models with different settings and sizes on the market. A thorough knowledge of how to use your specific air fryer is the key to success and will familiarize you with troubleshooting issues as well as safety functions. Read over the manual and wash all parts with warm, soapy water before first use to help you feel ready to unleash your culinary finesse.

Why Bake with an Air Fryer?

Air frying is increasingly popular because it allows you to quickly and evenly prepare delicious food with little effort. It's the perfect appliance for baking everything from cupcakes to fresh bread. Here are just a few of the reasons you'll want to switch to baking in your air fryer:

- **It replaces your oven.** You can use your air fryer in place of your oven, saving you time and energy costs, not to mention you'll no longer need to heat up your whole house just to make dessert. Using one small device, you can quickly bake perfect dishes without sacrifice.
- **It cooks faster than traditional cooking methods.** Air frying works by circulating hot air around the cooking chamber. This results in fast and even cooking, using a fraction of the energy of your oven. Most air fryers can be set to a maximum temperature of 400°F and a minimum temperature of about 180°F, so just about anything you can make in an oven, you can make in an air fryer.
- **Cleanup is fast.** Any method of cooking leaves a mess in your cooker, but your air fryer's smaller cooking chamber and removable basket make thorough cleanup a breeze!

Choosing an Air Fryer

When choosing an air fryer, the two most important factors to focus on are size and temperature range. Air fryers are usually measured by quart size, and range from about 1.2 quarts to 10 or more quarts. Thanks to the number of models available, you can now even find air fryer "ovens"—larger, convection oven–type appliances that you can use to cook multiple racks of food at the same time. These little ovens can be very convenient for baking larger dishes, but they're not completely necessary. This book is based on a basket-style air fryer with a 6-quart capacity. Depending on the functions you need, you'll want to make sure your air fryer has the appropriate cooking capacity and temperature range.

The Functions of an Air Fryer

Most air fryers are equipped with buttons to help you prepare food with baking, air frying, roasting, and reheating settings. These buttons are programmed to preset times and temperatures based on your specific air fryer. All the recipes in this book were created using manual times and temperatures and with an automatic preheat function. If yours doesn't have this function, allow 5 minutes at your desired temperature for preheating.

Essential Accessories

Your air fryer's cooking chamber is basically just a large, open space for the hot air to circulate. This is a huge advantage because it gives you the option to incorporate several different accessories into your cooking. These accessories broaden the number of recipes you can make in your air fryer and open up options you never would've thought were possible. Here are some of the best accessories for baking in your air fryer.

- **Foil baking cups.** These baking cups make it easy to bake cupcakes and muffins in your air fryer. They can also be helpful for preparing individual, pre-portioned treats and often work better than silicone baking cups.
- **Ramekins.** Small 4" ramekins are great for making mini cakes and quiches. If they're oven safe, they're safe to use in your air fryer.
- **Cake pans.** You can find specially made cake pans for your air fryer that fit perfectly into the cooking chamber; 6" cake pans are the perfect size for air fryer baking. They also often come with a built-in handle so you can easily pull them out when your cakes are done baking. You may need to look in the specialized bakeware sections, such as wedding cake decoration, to find these smaller pans. Aluminum pans of the same size also work great for these recipes.
- **Parchment.** Any parchment will work in the air fryer, but there are some ways to make this step even easier. Specially precut parchment can make cleanup even easier when baking with your air fryer. You want to be careful with using parchment because if it's not weighed down properly, the air fryer's fan can blow the lightweight paper up into the heating element and cause it to catch on fire. Alternatively, you can use vented silicone baking mats to create the same effect. These are heavier, and as an added benefit, they're reusable.

- **Cooking spray.** Although the air fryer cooks with little to no oil, there are some cases in which a little spray is essential. Especially in recipes that involve breading and flour, lightly spraying oil on the outside helps you get a browned exterior for a much tastier end product.
- **Aluminum foil.** Aluminum foil is safe for air fryers, and that's good news because it can be an excellent tool to help with your baking. Wrapping some recipes, like banana bread, in aluminum foil while baking can help the tops from browning too quickly. Sometimes, the heating element beating down directly on the food can lead to uneven cooking; that is, a perfectly golden brown top and a wet, undercooked middle. Aluminum foil can deflect some of the heat and help save your dishes from burning. Just make sure it's well secured to the pan. Aluminum foil is flimsy and can easily blow around your air fryer if not secured tightly enough.

Accessory Removal

Some pans can be more difficult to remove than others because of their size and the depth of the fryer basket. Here are some tools that will allow you to take items out of your appliance safely and easily.

- **Tongs.** These will be helpful when lifting hot treats in and out of the air fryer. Tongs are also useful for removing cooking pans that don't come with handles.
- **Oven mitts.** Sometimes simple is best. Your food will be very hot when you remove it, so it's great to have these around to protect your hands. Traditional oven mitts or even silicone mitts are both great options.

- **Flexible spatula.** Using a spatula in one hand to help you lift up the pan out of the basket, while holding on to the opposite side of the pan with an oven mitt can be an easy way to remove large pans that fill up most of the air fryer basket when it's hard to grab the sides carefully.

Cleaning Your Air Fryer

Before cleaning it, first ensure that your air fryer is completely cool and unplugged. To clean the air fryer pan, you'll need to:

1. Remove the air fryer pan from the base. Fill the pan with hot water and dish soap. Let the pan soak with the frying basket inside for 10 minutes.
2. Clean the basket thoroughly with a sponge or brush.
3. Remove the fryer basket and scrub the underside and outside walls.
4. Clean the air fryer pan with a sponge or brush.
5. Let everything air-dry and return to the air fryer base.

To clean the outside of your air fryer, simply wipe with a damp cloth. Then, be sure all components are in the correct position before beginning your next cooking adventure.

With this final information in hand, you are truly ready to get baking. Throughout the following chapters you'll find plenty of delicious recipes to suit all tastes. Use these recipes as your guide, and always feel free to adjust ingredients and flavors intuitively and customize dishes to your liking—just be aware that doing so will change the provided nutritional information.

Pies, Tarts, and Crisps

Who can resist the first bite into a deliciously flaky crust? Pies, tarts, and crisps are essential to the baking experience and prove that the outside layers are just as important, and mouthwateringly delicious, as the fillings you put inside. Even the most persistent sweet tooth can be calmed by the perfect crispy bite, and these recipes will be your go-to guide for whenever cravings strike. From lighter, fruity dishes to rich and indulgent desserts, this chapter's amazing recipes can please a crowd, or just be enjoyed by yourself. In the pages ahead, you'll find a range of sweet dishes that are quick to cook and serve, and even quicker to be devoured.

With recipes such as Peach Cobbler and Quick Mini S'mores Pies, you won't have to look further than this chapter for amazing pies to serve. Dessert time just got sweeter!

Easy Apple Crisp

This weeknight-friendly recipe uses premade pie filling and a pantry-based topping to make this dish easier than ever to prepare. The crispy golden topping provides a big crunch, which balances perfectly with soft, spiced apples. These contrasting textures will be sure to please everyone at the table.

Hands-on time: 10 minutes
Cook time: 8 minutes

Serves 6

1 (21-ounce) can apple pie filling
½ cup light brown sugar, packed
½ cup quick oats
½ cup all-purpose flour
¼ cup cold salted butter, cubed

PIE FILLING

If you don't like canned pie filling, feel free to use your own homemade recipe. As long as your filling is thick and its weight is approximately the same as the premade kind, this recipe will still turn out delicious. You can also add more spices to a canned pie filling to add your own twist.

1 Preheat air fryer to 350°F. Spray an 8" × 8" baking pan with cooking spray.

2 Pour pie filling into pan.

3 Place brown sugar, oats, flour, and butter into a food processor. Pulse eight times or until mixture becomes pea-sized balls. It should be able to stick together but not be overly dry or crumbly.

4 Sprinkle topping mixture over pie filling, using your fingers to press some topping pieces together into quarter-sized pieces before scattering them. Spray topping lightly with cooking spray.

5 Place pan into air fryer basket. Bake 8 minutes or until top is golden brown. For a crunchier topping, bake an extra 2 minutes or until top is dark golden brown. Serve warm.

PER SERVING

CALORIES: 299 | FAT: 8g | SODIUM: 112mg | CARBOHYDRATES: 56g | FIBER: 2g | SUGAR: 32g | PROTEIN: 2g

Peach Cobbler

Summer dessert has never been so quick and easy. This cobbler has a flat topping that is similar to a pie crust. The air fryer turns it a golden brown and ensures a delicious, flaky crunch in every bite. It's the perfect pairing with the sweetness of the peaches.

Hands-on time: 10 minutes
Cook time: 12 minutes

Serves 6

- 1 (16-ounce) can sliced peaches, drained
- 2 tablespoons granulated sugar, divided
- 1/2 cup light brown sugar, packed
- 1 teaspoon ground cinnamon
- 1/4 teaspoon ground nutmeg
- 1 1/2 teaspoons cornstarch
- 1 cup all-purpose flour
- 4 tablespoons salted butter, cubed and frozen
- 2 tablespoons whole milk

1 Preheat air fryer to 375°F. Spray an 8" × 8" baking pan with cooking spray.

2 In a medium bowl, mix peaches, 1 tablespoon granulated sugar, brown sugar, cinnamon, and nutmeg. Add cornstarch and stir until combined. Pour mixture in prepared pan.

3 Place flour and remaining 1 tablespoon granulated sugar into a food processor and pulse three times. Add butter and pulse six times, then slowly add milk. Pulse five more times or until mixture resembles sand-like texture.

4 Scatter dough pieces on top of peaches, evenly coating the top. Spray with cooking spray.

5 Place pan into air fryer basket. Bake 12 minutes or until top is browned and edges are bubbling. Serve warm.

PER SERVING

CALORIES: 282 | FAT: 8g | SODIUM: 72mg | CARBOHYDRATES: 51g | FIBER: 2g | SUGAR: 32g | PROTEIN: 3g

Quick Mini S'mores Pies

All of the ooey gooey fun of making s'mores by the campfire is brought inside, right to your air fryer. This scrumptious dessert features the perfect blend of rich and sweet flavors in individual mini pies. Each bite is filled with smooth chocolate ganache and a crumbly graham cracker crunch.

Hands-on time: 10 minutes

Cook time: 6 minutes

Yields 6, 1 per serving

- 1/4 cup heavy whipping cream
- 1/2 cup semisweet chocolate chips
- 6 (4") premade mini graham pie crusts
- 1 cup mini marshmallows

CUSTOMIZE IT

Chocolate chips are classic, but you can put your own spin on this recipe by using different types of chocolate. Dark chocolate squares or even chopped peanut butter cups make delicious alternatives.

1 Preheat air fryer to 300°F.

2 In a medium microwave-safe bowl, microwave heavy whipping cream 1 minute.

3 Quickly whisk chocolate chips into heavy whipping cream until melted.

4 Pour about 2 tablespoons chocolate mixture into each premade crust. Top with mini marshmallows.

5 Place pies into air fryer basket, working in batches as needed. Bake 5 minutes or until marshmallows begin to brown lightly.

6 Let pies cool 10 minutes on counter, then refrigerate at least 20 minutes until chilled.

PER SERVING

CALORIES: 233 | FAT: 12g | SODIUM: 122mg | CARBOHYDRATES: 30g | FIBER: 1g | SUGAR: 18g | PROTEIN: 2g

Blueberry Pie

Everything's better with a flaky crust, and this mouthwatering pie is the perfect way to use your blueberries. Get ready to serve up a slice of delight. The air fryer makes it easier than ever to create a full-sized, double-crust pie that everyone will love.

Hands-on time: 20 minutes
Cook time: 35 minutes

Serves 6

1 tablespoon all-purpose flour
2 (15-ounce) premade pie dough rounds
1 pound blueberries
3/4 cup granulated sugar
2 tablespoons cornstarch
2 tablespoons water
1/2 teaspoon ground cinnamon
1 tablespoon lemon juice
1 large egg, beaten
2 tablespoons sparkling sugar

1 Spray an 8" pie dish with cooking spray.

2 Dust a clean work surface with flour, then unroll dough on surface. Place 1 dough round into prepared dish, pressing so it comes up the sides.

3 In a small saucepan over medium heat, combine blueberries and granulated sugar. In a small bowl, whisk together cornstarch and water, then whisk mixture into blueberry mixture. Continue stirring until mixture begins to thicken and some blueberries begin to break down, about 5 minutes. It will be ready when you can scrape a spoon against bottom of pan and mixture doesn't immediately fill the space.

4 Add cinnamon and lemon juice to blueberry mixture and stir to combine. Remove from heat and let cool 5 minutes.

5 Preheat air fryer to 320°F.

6 Pour blueberry mixture into pie crust and cover with remaining dough round. Press edges down to seal.

7 Lightly brush egg over top of pie. Cut four 1" slits into the center of pie to allow it to vent. Sprinkle top with sparkling sugar.

8 Place pie into air fryer basket. Bake 30 minutes or until golden brown. Let cool at least 1 hour before serving.

PER SERVING

CALORIES: 493 | **FAT:** 17g | **SODIUM:** 302mg | **CARBOHYDRATES:** 79g | **FIBER:** 3g | **SUGAR:** 37g | **PROTEIN:** 4g

Mixed-Berry Hand Pies

Hand pies are incredibly convenient and bursting with all of the flavor of a full-sized pie. This recipe simplifies from-scratch pie-making with basic ingredients and straightforward instructions that even a beginner baker can follow. Give it a try; you may impress yourself!

Hands-on time: 20 minutes
Cook time: 27 minutes

Yields 8, 1 per serving

- ½ cup blueberries
- ½ cup raspberries
- 1 cup sliced strawberries
- ½ cup granulated sugar
- 2 tablespoons water
- 2 tablespoons cornstarch
- 1 tablespoon lemon juice
- 1 tablespoon all-purpose flour
- 1 (7-ounce) premade pie dough round
- 1 large egg, beaten
- 1 tablespoon sparkling sugar

BERRY COMBINATIONS

Feel free to change up the berry amounts or types to better suit your taste. You can completely omit blueberries and use equal parts blackberries, or simply add more raspberries if that's your preference. Frozen berry mixes will also work, but just be sure to thaw them before cooking.

1. In a small saucepan over medium heat, add blueberries, raspberries, strawberries, and granulated sugar. Stir to combine, using the back of a spoon to gently break down some of the berries, and bring to a gentle boil. Continue cooking about 10 minutes.

2. In a small bowl, whisk together water, cornstarch, and lemon juice. Pour into fruit mixture and allow 5 minutes to thicken over low heat.

3. Remove from heat and let cool 5 minutes.

4. Preheat air fryer to 350°F.

5. Dust a clean work surface with flour, then unroll dough and cut into four 5" rounds. You may need to gather dough after cutting and reroll out to get four more rounds.

6. Place 2 tablespoons fruit mixture into the center of each dough round. Fold over to close and use a fork to press edges together.

7. Brush egg over top of pies, then sprinkle with sparkling sugar.

8. Place pies into the air fryer basket, working in batches as needed. Bake 12 minutes, flipping after 8 minutes. Pies will be done when golden brown and firm. Let cool at least 10 minutes before serving.

PER SERVING

CALORIES: 196 | FAT: 6g | SODIUM: 110mg | CARBOHYDRATES: 32g | FIBER: 2g | SUGAR: 16g | PROTEIN: 2g

Caramel Banana Hand Pies

This recipe is like bananas Foster you can hold in your hand (no fire necessary!). This is a great last-minute recipe to use up bananas that are overripe. To take this recipe to the next level, try topping with a scoop of vanilla ice cream and a drizzle of caramel on top.

Hands-on time: 15 minutes
Cook time: 20 minutes

Yields 8, 1 per serving

- 2 tablespoons all-purpose flour, for dusting
- 1 (15-ounce) box frozen premade pie dough, thawed
- 1 medium banana, peeled and cut into 32 slices
- 1/4 cup light brown sugar, packed
- 2 tablespoons heavy whipping cream
- 1/2 teaspoon ground cinnamon
- 1 large egg, whisked

1. Preheat air fryer to 350°F.

2. Dust a clean work surface with flour, then unroll dough. Cut into sixteen 4" rounds. You will need to gather dough scraps and roll out to get the full number.

3. Place 4 banana slices on each of eight dough rounds.

4. In a small bowl, whisk together brown sugar, heavy whipping cream, and cinnamon. Place 2 teaspoons mixture over banana slices on each pie.

5. Top each pie with a remaining dough round and press edges together to seal. Gently press together with a fork if necessary. Brush each pie with egg.

6. Place pies into air fryer basket, working in batches as needed. Bake 10 minutes, flipping after 8 minutes. The pies will be done when crust is golden brown. Let cool at least 10 minutes before serving.

PER SERVING

CALORIES: 333 | FAT: 16g | SODIUM: 260mg | CARBOHYDRATES: 41g | FIBER: 2g | SUGAR: 11g | PROTEIN: 5g

Mini Lemon Tarts

If you love the filling of lemon bars but like a little crunch in your dessert, this recipe is perfect for you. The creamy lemon filling is delicious on top of the flaky pastry dough. Baked in foil baking liners, these tarts are great for making desserts ahead of time, or just keeping a quick treat to enjoy throughout the week.

Hands-on time: 10 minutes
Cook time: 12 minutes

Yields 12, 1 per serving

2 (13.2-ounce) packages frozen puff pastry, thawed
4 large egg yolks
½ cup fresh lemon juice
2 teaspoons lemon zest
1 (14-ounce) can sweetened condensed milk

1 Preheat air fryer to 320°F. Spray twelve foil baking liners with cooking spray.

2 Cut twelve 4" circles out of puff pastry. Place puff pastry circles into prepared liners, then poke the center of each puff pastry piece with a fork.

3 In a medium bowl, whisk together egg yolks, lemon juice, lemon zest, and sweetened condensed milk. Place 2 tablespoons mixture in each baking liner on top of puff pastry circle.

4 Place liners into air fryer basket, working in batches as needed. Bake 12 minutes or until puff pastry is browned and filling has set. Let tarts cool 20 minutes, then chill in refrigerator at least 1 hour before serving.

PER SERVING

CALORIES: 470 | FAT: 27g | SODIUM: 199mg | CARBOHYDRATES: 47g | FIBER: 1g | SUGAR: 19g | PROTEIN: 8g

Mini Pear Tarts

These tarts are light, flaky, and just the right amount of sweet. When executed correctly, they look and taste like you picked them up from your local bakery. Every bite is filled with a sweet taste of fresh pear and a crunch from honey-sweetened toasted almonds.

Hands-on time: 15 minutes
Cook time: 15 minutes

Yields 6, 1 per serving

1 (13.2-ounce) package frozen puff pastry, thawed
3 tablespoons light brown sugar, packed
3 medium Bartlett pears, peeled
1 large egg, whisked
1/2 teaspoon ground nutmeg
3 tablespoons honey
6 tablespoons sliced almonds

1 Preheat air fryer to 350°F. Cut a piece of parchment to fit air fryer basket.

2 Unroll puff pastry and cut into six equal pieces, then place on parchment.

3 Make an X on each pastry piece using a knife. Place 1/2 tablespoon brown sugar in the center of each X.

4 Cut top and bottom off each pear. Slice pears in half lengthwise, then use a spoon to remove cores. Cut each pear half into 1/4"-thick slices, keeping slices for each pear half together. Place slices from each pear half on a pastry piece.

5 Lightly brush each tart with egg, then sprinkle with nutmeg.

6 Place parchment with tarts into air fryer basket, working in batches as needed. Bake 12 minutes or until puff pastry is golden brown and pears are tender.

7 Drizzle honey over tarts while cooling.

8 In a small skillet over medium heat, toast almonds 3 minutes or until warmed and just beginning to turn brown. Sprinkle over tarts to serve.

PER SERVING

CALORIES: 503 | FAT: 26g | SODIUM: 172mg | CARBOHYDRATES: 58g | FIBER: 3g | SUGAR: 25g | PROTEIN: 7g

Banana Tarte Tatin

Your guests will have no idea that this elegant dessert came together in just minutes! Rich with the flavor of caramelized bananas, and perfectly sweet, Banana Tarte Tatin is sure to impress. Don't forget to add a scoop of ice cream for good measure!

Hands-on time: 15 minutes
Cook time: 19 minutes

Serves 4

¼ cup salted butter
¼ cup light brown sugar, packed
½ teaspoon ground cinnamon
¼ teaspoon ground nutmeg
2 medium bananas, peeled, ends removed
1 (13.2-ounce) package frozen puff pastry, thawed

1 In a small saucepan over medium heat, melt butter and brown sugar, about 2 minutes. Stir in cinnamon and nutmeg and stir continuously until mixture begins to thicken and bubble, about 5 minutes. Continue stirring until sauce is thick enough to coat the back of a spoon. Remove from heat.

2 Preheat air fryer to 350°F. Spray a 6" round baking pan with cooking spray.

3 Cut bananas in half horizontally, then in half vertically. Arrange in prepared pan, cutting banana pieces as needed to cover bottom of pan.

4 Pour caramel sauce evenly over bananas.

5 Cut a 6" circle out of puff pastry, then use a fork to poke holes in it to prevent excess rising. Place puff pastry round on top of bananas and caramel.

6 Place pan into air fryer basket. Bake 12 minutes or until puff pastry is golden brown and caramel is bubbling slightly over edges of puff pastry.

7 Let cool in pan 5 minutes, then place a medium plate over top of pan. Carefully flip upside down to release onto plate. Let cool 10 additional minutes, then serve.

PER SERVING

CALORIES: 722 | FAT: 45g | SODIUM: 328mg | CARBOHYDRATES: 70g | FIBER: 3g | SUGAR: 21g | PROTEIN: 8g

Apple Pie

It doesn't get much more classic than a homemade apple pie. This recipe uses Honeycrisp apples because they are sweet with just a hint of tartness.

Hands-on time: 20 minutes
Cook time: 45 minutes

Serves 6

1/2 cup plus 2 tablespoons light brown sugar, packed, divided

1 teaspoon ground cinnamon, divided

1 cup water

1 tablespoon lemon juice

1/4 cup cornstarch

2 large Honeycrisp apples, cored and thinly sliced

1 tablespoon all-purpose flour

2 (8") premade pie dough rounds

1 large egg, beaten

1 In a small saucepan over medium heat, add 1/2 cup brown sugar, 1/2 teaspoon cinnamon, water, and lemon juice and whisk to combine. Bring to a boil, stirring occasionally.

2 Whisk in cornstarch until fully incorporated. Add apples and stir to coat. Lower heat to a simmer and cook until apples have softened, about 5 minutes. Remove from heat and let cool for 5 minutes.

3 Preheat air fryer to 320°F. Spray a 6" pie dish with cooking spray.

4 Dust a clean work surface with flour and unroll dough rounds. Place 1 dough round into prepared dish, pressing so it comes up the sides.

5 Sprinkle 1 tablespoon brown sugar and remaining 1/2 teaspoon cinnamon on bottom crust.

6 Pour cooled apple mixture in dish and use a spoon to make a single layer. Top with remaining dough round and press edges together to seal.

7 Brush egg over top of pie and sprinkle with remaining 1 tablespoon brown sugar. Cut four slits into top of pie for venting.

8 Place pie into air fryer basket. Bake 40 minutes or until top is browned and filling is bubbling. Let cool at least 4 hours before serving.

PER SERVING

CALORIES: 457 | FAT: 16g | SODIUM: 291mg | CARBOHYDRATES: 72g | FIBER: 3g | SUGAR: 29g | PROTEIN: 3g

Blackberry Crumb Pie

If you're a fan of crunchy crumble topping and also flaky pie crust, this recipe is for you. It combines two delicious elements to put a unique spin on a fruit-filled dessert. If blackberries aren't your thing, feel free to use a can of cherry or blueberry pie filling instead.

Hands-on time: 15 minutes
Cook time: 25 minutes

Serves 8

1 (8") frozen premade pie crust, thawed
1 (21-ounce) can blackberry pie filling
1 teaspoon lemon juice
1 tablespoon granulated sugar
4 tablespoons salted butter, softened
$1/3$ cup light brown sugar, packed
$1/2$ cup all-purpose flour
$1/4$ teaspoon vanilla extract
$1/4$ teaspoon almond extract

1 Preheat air fryer to 350°F.

2 Place premade crust into air fryer basket and bake 5 minutes or until golden.

3 In a medium bowl, mix pie filling, lemon juice, and granulated sugar. Pour mixture into baked pie crust.

4 In a separate medium bowl, mix butter, brown sugar, flour, vanilla, and almond extract with a fork until mixture becomes large crumbs with a sand-like consistency. Sprinkle mixture evenly on top of pie filling.

5 Place pie into air fryer basket. Bake 20 minutes or until pie filling is bubbling and crumb topping is golden brown. Let cool at least 2 hours before serving.

PER SERVING

CALORIES: 298 | FAT: 10g | SODIUM: 145mg | CARBOHYDRATES: 46g | FIBER: 3g | SUGAR: 26g | PROTEIN: 2g

Mini Pecan Pies

This one is a Southern classic, in bite-sized form! These mini pies are both sweet and savory, and bursting with pecans. This recipe is great for a party because guests can grab one and continue to mingle; no need to sit down with a fork and knife.

Hands-on time: 15 minutes
Cook time: 15 minutes

Yields 8, 1 per serving

¼ cup dark corn syrup
¼ cup light brown sugar, packed
2 tablespoons salted butter, softened
1 large egg
2 teaspoons vanilla extract
1 (15-ounce) box premade pie dough
1 cup pecans, chopped

1 Preheat air fryer to 320°F. Spray eight foil baking liners with cooking spray.

2 In a medium bowl, combine corn syrup, brown sugar, butter, egg, and vanilla.

3 Unroll pie dough and cut out eight 4" circles. Place each dough round into a prepared liner.

4 Place 2 tablespoons pecans on top of each dough round. Pour 2 tablespoons corn syrup mixture in each liner.

5 Place pies into air fryer basket, working in batches as needed. Bake 15 minutes or until crust is golden brown and pies are set on edges and in the center. Let cool completely, at least 1 hour, before serving.

PER SERVING

CALORIES: 423 | **FAT:** 25g | **SODIUM:** 266mg | **CARBOHYDRATES:** 44g | **FIBER:** 2g | **SUGAR:** 15g | **PROTEIN:** 4g

Chocolate Pecan Pie

If you thought pecan pie couldn't get any more delicious, think again! This twist on the classic version is perfect for chocolate lovers. The addition of chocolate chips makes it decadently creamy and adds a whole new layer of flavor to this tasty dessert.

Hands-on time: 15 minutes
Cook time: 30 minutes

Serves 8

½ cup light corn syrup
½ cup light brown sugar, packed
¼ cup salted butter, melted
1 teaspoon vanilla extract
2 large egg yolks
½ cup semisweet chocolate chips
1 cup chopped pecans
1 (8") frozen premade pie crust, thawed

1 Preheat air fryer to 320°F.

2 In a medium bowl, mix corn syrup, brown sugar, butter, and vanilla until fully combined.

3 Stir in egg yolks until fully combined.

4 Fold in chocolate chips and pecans, then pour mixture into crust.

5 Place pie into air fryer basket. Bake 30 minutes or until top is set and a knife inserted into the center comes out clean. Let pie cool at least 6 hours until fully cooled and firm before serving.

PER SERVING

CALORIES: 424 | FAT: 24g | SODIUM: 155mg | CARBOHYDRATES: 50g | FIBER: 3g | SUGAR: 38g | PROTEIN: 4g

Mini Sweet Potato Pies

This recipe is perfect for holiday gatherings or when you just want to enjoy a mini festive treat at home. Top these deliciously flaky and sweet pies with whipped cream and a light sprinkle of cinnamon for a crowd-pleasing presentation.

Hands-on time: 15 minutes
Cook time: 12 minutes

Yields 24, 2 per serving

1 (15-ounce) can sweet potatoes in syrup, drained
$^1\!/_4$ cup salted butter, softened
$^1\!/_2$ cup light brown sugar, packed
$^1\!/_4$ cup sweetened condensed milk
1 large egg
$^1\!/_4$ teaspoon ground nutmeg
$^1\!/_2$ teaspoon ground cinnamon
1 teaspoon vanilla extract
2 (8") frozen premade pie dough rounds, thawed

1   Preheat air fryer to 350°F. Spray twenty-four foil mini baking liners with cooking spray.

2   In a large bowl, mash drained sweet potatoes until smooth. Mix in butter, brown sugar, and sweetened condensed milk until well combined. Stir in egg, nutmeg, cinnamon, and vanilla.

3   Unroll dough and cut out twenty-four 4" circles. You will need to gather dough pieces and roll them out to get the full yield.

4   Place each dough circle in a baking liner, gently pressing toward the bottom.

5   Place 1 heaping tablespoonful sweet potato mixture in each liner on top of dough.

6   Place pies into air fryer basket, working in batches as needed. Bake 12 minutes or until crust is golden brown and filling is lightly browned and set. Let cool at least 1 hour before serving.

PER SERVING

CALORIES: 128 | FAT: 6g | SODIUM: 88mg | CARBOHYDRATES: 17g | FIBER: 1g | SUGAR: 8g | PROTEIN: 2g

Cinnamon Oatmeal Pie

You may have never heard of oatmeal pie, but its warm comfort food feel will win you over! If you love soft oatmeal cookies, this pie is a must. Just a hint of spice makes this pie taste like a chewy cookie in a delicious, flaky crust.

Hands-on time: 15 minutes
Cook time: 25 minutes

Serves 8

½ cup light brown sugar, packed
½ cup light corn syrup
1 teaspoon vanilla extract
½ teaspoon salt
1 tablespoon ground cinnamon
1 cup quick oats
2 large egg yolks
1 (8") frozen premade pie crust, thawed

1 Preheat air fryer to 320°F.

2 In a medium bowl, mix brown sugar, corn syrup, vanilla, salt, and cinnamon until well combined.

3 Mix in oats and egg yolks until fully combined. Pour mixture in pie crust.

4 Place pie into air fryer basket. Bake 25 minutes or until a toothpick inserted into the center comes out clean. Let cool 2 hours before serving.

PER SERVING

CALORIES: 266 | FAT: 7g | SODIUM: 254mg | CARBOHYDRATES: 49g | FIBER: 2g | SUGAR: 31g | PROTEIN: 3g

CUSTOMIZE IT
Want to take this dish to the next level? Try adding ¼ cup dried fruit or milk chocolate chips for a flavorful spin on this recipe. Alternatively, you can add a chocolate drizzle on top for a decadent bite.

Mini Chocolate Caramel Pies

The filling is smooth and silky, but the crust provides this decadent dessert with just the right amount of crunch. For an extra-special treat, feel free to top one of these pies with whipped cream.

Hands-on time: 16 minutes
Cook time: 8 minutes

Yields 6, 1 per serving

1/2 cup heavy whipping cream
1 cup semisweet chocolate chips
2 large egg yolks
1/2 teaspoon vanilla extract
12 tablespoons caramel sauce
6 (4") premade mini graham pie crusts

1 Preheat air fryer to 320°F.

2 In a medium microwave-safe bowl, microwave heavy whipping cream 1 minute. Whisk in chocolate chips until fully melted.

3 Whisk in egg yolks and vanilla until smooth.

4 Place 2 tablespoons caramel sauce in each pie crust. Pour chocolate mixture over caramel, about 3 tablespoons in each pie.

5 Place pies into air fryer basket, working in batches as needed. Bake 8 minutes or until edges are set and the center jiggles only slightly. Let cool 10 minutes, then refrigerate 1 hour. Serve chilled.

PER SERVING

CALORIES: 436 | **FAT:** 22g | **SODIUM:** 266mg | **CARBOHYDRATES:** 60g | **FIBER:** 2g | **SUGAR:** 22g | **PROTEIN:** 4g

Blackberry Crisp

This old-fashioned dessert has an ultra-crunchy oat topping in every bite! If you have other berries such as raspberries or blueberries, feel free to add those in to make this a triple-berry crisp. This recipe is perfect for using up berries that have gone a bit soft because they make the dish extra saucy and delicious.

Hands-on time: 10 minutes
Cook time: 15 minutes

Serves 4

2 cups blackberries
1 tablespoon cornstarch
$\frac{1}{2}$ cup granulated sugar
$\frac{1}{2}$ cup all-purpose flour
1 cup old-fashioned oats
$\frac{1}{2}$ cup light brown sugar, packed
$\frac{1}{4}$ teaspoon salt
$\frac{1}{4}$ teaspoon ground cinnamon
3 tablespoons salted butter, melted

1 Preheat air fryer to 350°F. Spray an 8" × 8" baking pan with cooking spray.

2 In a large bowl, toss blackberries with cornstarch and granulated sugar. Pour mixture in prepared pan, using your hands or a fork to break blackberries into pieces and press into a single layer.

3 Place flour, oats, brown sugar, salt, and cinnamon into a food processor and pulse five times. Add butter and pulse ten times or until mixture is the consistency of wet sand and sticks together when pressed between your fingers.

4 Sprinkle flour mixture over blackberries, pressing some pieces together to make larger bits.

5 Place pan into air fryer basket. Bake 15 minutes or until top is golden brown and berry sauce is bubbling. Let cool for 10 minutes before serving. Serve warm.

PER SERVING

CALORIES: 467 | FAT: 10g | SODIUM: 222mg | CARBOHYDRATES: 89g | FIBER: 7g | SUGAR: 56g | PROTEIN: 6g

Blueberry Crumble

This easy recipe doesn't take much prep and cooks quickly, meaning you'll be enjoying a delicious dessert before you know it. The lemon juice is the secret ingredient in this recipe because it adds just the right amount of tang to the fruit to brighten the whole dish. Try it warm with a scoop of vanilla ice cream!

Hands-on time: 15 minutes
Cook time: 10 minutes

Serves 4

3 cups blueberries
3/4 cup granulated sugar, divided
1 teaspoon vanilla extract
1 tablespoon lemon juice
1/2 tablespoon cornstarch
1/4 teaspoon salt
2 tablespoons light brown sugar, packed
3/4 cup all-purpose flour
4 tablespoons salted butter, melted
1/2 teaspoon ground cinnamon

1 Preheat air fryer to 320°F. Spray a 6" round baking pan with cooking spray.

2 In a large bowl, toss blueberries, 1/2 cup granulated sugar, and vanilla.

3 In a small bowl, whisk together lemon juice and cornstarch and pour into blueberry mixture, then stir to coat blueberries. Pour blueberry mixture into prepared pan.

4 In a medium bowl, mix remaining 1/4 cup granulated sugar, salt, brown sugar, flour, butter, and cinnamon until coarse crumbs form. Spread mixture on top of berry mixture.

5 Place pan into air fryer basket. Bake 10 minutes or until top is golden brown and filling is bubbling. Let cool at least 20 minutes for filling to thicken before serving.

PER SERVING

CALORIES: 429 | **FAT:** 11g | **SODIUM:** 385mg | **CARBOHYDRATES:** 80g | **FIBER:** 3g | **SUGAR:** 55g | **PROTEIN:** 3g

Buttermilk Pie

You may not think of buttermilk when you think of a pie, but buttermilk is actually the perfect addition to this sweet and buttery pie. This is a custard-style pie, so if you like crème brûlée, this might just be your new favorite dessert!

Hands-on time: 15 minutes
Cook time: 25 minutes

Serves 8

- ¼ cup salted butter, softened
- ½ cup granulated sugar
- ¼ cup light brown sugar, packed
- 2 large egg yolks
- ½ cup buttermilk, at room temperature
- ½ teaspoon vanilla extract
- 1 tablespoon cornstarch
- 2 tablespoons all-purpose flour
- 1 (9") frozen premade pie crust, thawed
- ¼ teaspoon ground nutmeg

1 Preheat air fryer to 320°F.

2 In a large bowl, use an electric hand mixer to beat butter, granulated sugar, and brown sugar until light and fluffy, about 2 minutes.

3 Add egg yolks and buttermilk and mix until well combined. Add vanilla and cornstarch and mix. Add flour and mix until mixture is thin and very pourable. Pour mixture in pie crust.

4 Place pie into air fryer basket. Bake 25 minutes or until top is golden brown. Sprinkle top with nutmeg, then let cool 30 minutes before putting in refrigerator to chill at least 2 hours. Serve chilled.

PER SERVING

CALORIES: 257 | FAT: 12g | SODIUM: 155mg | CARBOHYDRATES: 33g | FIBER: 1g | SUGAR: 21g | PROTEIN: 3g

Pumpkin Pie

There's nothing like a classic! Now with your air fryer, dessert can bake even if the oven is full with dinner. Feel free to swap the ginger and cloves for 1 tablespoon of pumpkin pie spice if that's what you have on hand. This smooth, spice-packed pie is the perfect addition to any fall meal.

Hands-on time: 10 minutes
Cook time: 25 minutes

Serves 6

1 (15-ounce) can pumpkin purée
1 tablespoon ground cinnamon
1 teaspoon ground ginger
$\frac{1}{2}$ teaspoon ground cloves
$\frac{1}{2}$ teaspoon salt
1 large egg
1 teaspoon vanilla extract
1 (14-ounce) can sweetened condensed milk
1 (8") premade graham cracker pie crust

1 Preheat air fryer to 325°F.

2 In a large bowl, whisk together pumpkin purée, cinnamon, ginger, cloves, salt, egg, vanilla, and sweetened condensed milk until well combined. Pour mixture into pie crust.

3 Place pie in air fryer basket. Bake 25 minutes or until pie is lightly brown and firm, and a toothpick inserted into the center comes out clean. Chill in refrigerator until set, at least 2 hours, before serving.

PER SERVING

CALORIES: 401 | FAT: 13g | SODIUM: 426mg | CARBOHYDRATES: 62g | FIBER: 3g | SUGAR: 44g | PROTEIN: 8g

PURE PUMPKIN

When you're grocery shopping, be sure to look for 100 percent pure pumpkin for this recipe. This isn't the same as pumpkin pie filling, which you may also see on the shelf. Pumpkin pie filling has added spices and sugar and isn't a direct swap in this recipe.

Brown Sugar Pie

The pie's texture is similar to pecan pie's, but without the nuts. And it would taste delicious with a big scoop of whipped cream on top.

Hands-on time: 15 minutes
Cook time: 20 minutes

Serves 8

1 cup light brown sugar, packed
2 tablespoons all-purpose flour
2 large egg yolks
$1/4$ cup salted butter, melted
2 teaspoons vanilla extract
$1/2$ cup evaporated milk
1 (9") frozen premade pie crust, thawed

1 Preheat air fryer to 320°F.

2 In a medium bowl, whisk together brown sugar, flour, egg yolks, butter, vanilla, and evaporated milk until smooth. Pour mixture in pie crust.

3 Place pie into air fryer basket. Bake 20 minutes or until top is firm, and a knife inserted into the center comes out clean. Let cool at least 4 hours before serving.

PER SERVING

CALORIES: 298 | FAT: 13g | SODIUM: 161mg | CARBOHYDRATES: 41g | FIBER: 1g | SUGAR: 28g | PROTEIN: 3g

Coconut Custard Pie

This creamy pie is mildly flavored, so even those who aren't coconut superfans can still enjoy it. If you like citrus, try adding 1 tablespoon orange or lime zest to this pie for a twist on the flavor.

Hands-on time: 15 minutes
Cook time: 20 minutes

Serves 8

2 large eggs
2 large egg yolks
$1/4$ cup granulated sugar
$1/3$ cup light brown sugar, packed
1 teaspoon vanilla extract
$1/4$ teaspoon salt
1 (13.5-ounce) can full-fat coconut milk
3 tablespoons cornstarch
$1/2$ cup sweetened shredded coconut
1 (9") frozen premade pie crust, thawed

1 Preheat air fryer to 300°F.

2 In a large bowl, whisk together eggs, egg yolks, granulated sugar, brown sugar, vanilla, and salt until well combined.

3 Whisk in coconut milk, cornstarch, and coconut until well combined, then pour mixture in crust.

4 Place pie into air fryer basket. Bake 20 minutes or until top is golden brown. Let cool at least 1 hour before serving.

PER SERVING

CALORIES: 319 | FAT: 18g | SODIUM: 206mg | CARBOHYDRATES: 33g | FIBER: 1g | SUGAR: 18g | PROTEIN: 5g

Strawberry Crisp

This recipe is easy and ready in less than 30 minutes! Fresh strawberries taste best when they aren't overcooked, which makes the air fryer perfect for this recipe. The top crisps up quickly, and the strawberries stay soft and juicy without losing all their vibrant flavor.

Hands-on time: 10 minutes
Cook time: 10 minutes

Yields 4, 1 per serving

12 ounces strawberries, hulled and chopped
2 teaspoons lemon juice
2 teaspoons granulated sugar
2 teaspoons cornstarch
1/4 cup old-fashioned oats
1/4 cup all-purpose flour
1/4 cup light brown sugar, packed
1/4 teaspoon ground cinnamon
1/4 cup salted butter, cubed

FRESH STRAWBERRIES

For the best taste, use fresh strawberries for this recipe. Canned strawberry filling is not a good substitute due to the excess syrup. You can swap for equal amounts frozen strawberries, but be sure to let them thaw first. You can place them in a bowl on the counter until thawed, or run under cool water to help speed up the process.

1 Preheat air fryer to 350°F. Spray four 4" ramekins with cooking spray.

2 In a large bowl, toss strawberries, lemon juice, and granulated sugar. Let sit 10 minutes.

3 Pour juice from bowl with strawberries into a medium bowl, then add cornstarch and whisk until well combined. Pour mixture back into bowl with strawberries.

4 Place remaining ingredients into a food processor and pulse ten times or until butter is broken down and mixture begins to form crumbs.

5 Distribute strawberries evenly among prepared ramekins. Top each ramekin with equal amounts crumb mixture.

6 Place ramekins into air fryer basket. Bake 10 minutes or until topping is golden brown and filling is bubbling around edges. Let cool 10 minutes before serving. The topping will crisp as it cools.

PER SERVING

CALORIES: 244 | FAT: 11g | SODIUM: 20mg | CARBOHYDRATES: 33g | FIBER: 3g | SUGAR: 20g | PROTEIN: 2g

Cranberry Sour Cream Pie

Cranberries don't get used in pie as often as other fruits, but don't let their naturally bitter nature deter you. They are very easy to work with and sweeten up easily with sugar, and give this pie a delicious tartness that brightens up the entire dish. If you prefer not to make the pecan pie crust this recipe includes, you can simply use a regular premade crust with no additional changes.

Hands-on time: 15 minutes
Cook time: 20 minutes

Serves 8

2 cups pecans
2 tablespoons salted butter
1/4 cup plus 1 tablespoon light brown sugar, packed, divided
2 large eggs
1 large egg yolk
1/4 cup granulated sugar
1/2 cup sour cream
2 teaspoons vanilla extract
2 tablespoons all-purpose flour
1/2 cup cranberries

FRUIT SWAP

If you aren't a fan of cranberries, that doesn't mean you need to miss out on this recipe. If that's the case, you can simply swap them out for equal parts raspberries or blueberries, which will provide a sweeter flavor.

1 Preheat air fryer to 350°F. Spray an 8" pie dish with cooking spray.

2 Place pecans, butter, and 1 tablespoon brown sugar into a food processor. Process 15 seconds or until mixture sticks together.

3 Press mixture in prepared pie dish, then place dish into air fryer basket and bake 5 minutes.

4 In a large bowl, whisk together remaining 1/4 cup brown sugar, eggs, egg yolk, granulated sugar, sour cream, and vanilla until well combined. Stir in flour and cranberries. Pour mixture in baked pie crust.

5 Place pie into air fryer basket. Bake 15 minutes or until top is golden and center jiggles only slightly. Let cool on counter 2 hours, then place in refrigerator to chill at least 4 hours to cool completely. Serve chilled.

PER SERVING

CALORIES: 318 | FAT: 24g | SODIUM: 50mg | CARBOHYDRATES: 21g | FIBER: 3g | SUGAR: 16g | PROTEIN: 5g

3

Pastries and Scones

Who doesn't love to stop by the bakery or coffee shop on the way to work for a little pick-me-up in the morning? This chapter will teach you how to re-create some of your bakery favorites and introduce you to some new ones, and they all can be made right at home in your air fryer!

Pastries and scones are amazing because they can be enjoyed for either breakfast or dessert. They also can be as rich or as light as you want them to be, and you can always customize the spices and mix-ins to your liking using simple tweaks or substitutions. With recipes from Lemon Poppy Seed Scones to Triple-Berry Danish, this chapter is loaded with sweet recipes for every level of baking experience!

Pumpkin Spice Scones

These scones just taste like fall. The burst of pumpkin flavor is the perfect complement for cool, crisp mornings, and the pumpkin pie spice adds just the right amount of warmth. This recipe is also egg-free, as pumpkin purée can be used as an egg substitute in many baking recipes.

Hands-on time: 16 minutes
Cook time: 30 minutes

Yields 8, 1 per serving

- 1/2 cup cold salted butter, divided
- 2 cups plus 2 tablespoons all-purpose flour, divided
- 1/2 cup light brown sugar, packed
- 1/2 teaspoon baking powder
- 2 1/2 teaspoons pumpkin pie spice
- 3/4 cup pumpkin purée
- 5 tablespoons whole milk
- 2 ounces cream cheese, softened
- 1/4 cup confectioners' sugar
- 2 tablespoons heavy whipping cream

1 Preheat air fryer to 320°F. Cut two or three pieces of parchment to fit air fryer basket.

2 Place 6 tablespoons butter in freezer 10 minutes. In a small microwave-safe bowl, melt remaining 2 tablespoons butter in 30-second increments.

3 In a large bowl, mix 2 cups flour, brown sugar, baking powder, and pumpkin pie spice.

4 Remove butter from freezer and grate into flour mixture. Use a wooden spoon to evenly distribute.

5 Add pumpkin purée and milk and stir gently until a soft, sticky dough forms.

6 Dust a clean work surface with remaining 2 tablespoons flour and scoop dough onto surface. Fold a couple times and gently form into an 8" round. Cut into eight triangles and place on parchment.

7 Brush each piece with melted butter. Place parchment into air fryer basket, working in batches as needed.

8 Bake 15 minutes or until scones are dark golden brown, and a toothpick inserted in the middle of each scone comes out clean.

9 To make the glaze, combine cream cheese, confectioners' sugar, and heavy whipping cream in a small bowl until smooth. Drizzle glaze over each scone before serving.

PER SERVING

CALORIES: 333 | FAT: 15g | SODIUM: 158mg | CARBOHYDRATES: 44g | FIBER: 1g | SUGAR: 18g | PROTEIN: 4g

Cinnamon Rolls

These made-from-scratch Cinnamon Rolls are worth the effort! Most of the prep involves letting the dough rise, which means you won't be spending hours in the kitchen.

Hands-on time: 30 minutes
Cook time: 30 minutes

Yields 9, 1 per serving

- ½ cup lukewarm whole milk
- 2 teaspoons active yeast
- ½ cup granulated sugar, divided
- 2½ cups plus 4 tablespoons all-purpose flour, divided
- ½ teaspoon salt
- 2 large eggs, whisked
- ⅓ cup salted butter, softened
- ¼ cup light brown sugar, packed
- 1½ tablespoons ground cinnamon
- 4 ounces cream cheese, softened
- ½ cup confectioners' sugar
- 4 tablespoons heavy whipping cream

1. In a medium bowl, add milk, yeast, and ¼ cup granulated sugar and gently stir. Let yeast activate 10 minutes; it should look foamy and bubbles will form.

2. In a large bowl, mix 2½ cups flour and salt. Pour in yeast mixture and stir until combined. Add eggs and stir until well combined.

3. Dust a clean work surface with 2 tablespoons flour, and knead dough 10 minutes or until smooth and elastic. Shape into a ball. Lightly spray a clean large bowl with cooking spray and add dough ball to bowl. Cover bowl with plastic wrap. Let dough rise 2 hours.

4. Dust a clean work surface with remaining 2 tablespoons flour and roll dough out to a 9" × 12" rectangle, about ½" thick.

5. Spread butter on dough rectangle, then sprinkle with remaining ¼ cup granulated sugar and brown sugar. Sprinkle cinnamon across dough and gently press in.

6. Roll dough up lengthwise, leaving a 9"-long roll. Carefully slice into nine 1" pieces. Let rise 15 minutes. Preheat air fryer to 320°F.

7. Place rolls into air fryer basket, working in batches. Bake 15 minutes or until golden brown. Let cool 5 minutes before serving.

8. To make the glaze, whisk cream cheese, confectioners' sugar and heavy whipping cream in a small bowl until smooth. Serve drizzled over cinnamon rolls.

PER SERVING

CALORIES: 370 | FAT: 14g | SODIUM: 256mg | CARBOHYDRATES: 52g | FIBER: 2g | SUGAR: 24g | PROTEIN: 7g

Easy Strawberry Sweet Rolls

These sweet fruit rolls are bursting with flavor. The bread dough tastes similar to cinnamon roll dough, but using frozen dough cuts down on prep time. This fresh take mixes fruit preserves and fresh fruit for the perfect balance of sweet and tart. These rolls make the perfect companion for a cup of coffee.

Hands-on time: 10 minutes
Cook time: 30 minutes

Yields 12, 1 per serving

1 (16-ounce) premade frozen bread dough, thawed
½ cup strawberry preserves
6 medium strawberries, hulled and chopped
1 tablespoon unsalted butter, softened
½ cup confectioners' sugar
2 tablespoons whole milk

1 Preheat air fryer to 320°F. Spray an 8" × 8" baking dish with cooking spray.

2 Unroll dough on a clean work surface and roll into a 10" × 12" rectangle.

3 Spread preserves on dough, then scatter strawberries on top. Roll dough up width-wise, leaving a 12"-long roll.

4 Slice roll into twelve even pieces and place in prepared baking dish. Place dish into air fryer basket, working in batches as needed. Bake 15 minutes or until rolls are browned. Let cool 10 minutes.

5 To make the glaze, whisk together butter, confectioners' sugar, and milk in a small bowl until smooth. Drizzle glaze over rolls before serving.

PER SERVING

CALORIES: 158 | FAT: 2g | SODIUM: 226mg | CARBOHYDRATES: 32g | FIBER: 1g | SUGAR: 13g | PROTEIN: 3g

Orange Scones

Making scones at home is easier than you think. These sweet biscuits bake beautifully in the air fryer. The flaky layers get crunchy and sweet on the edges, but the insides are tender and buttery. The buttermilk gives these scones just a little tang, which is extra delicious alongside the orange cream flavor.

Hands-on time: 10 minutes
Cook time: 30 minutes

Yields 6, 1 per serving

- 2 cups plus 2 tablespoons self-rising flour, divided
- 1/4 teaspoon salt
- 1/3 cup light brown sugar, packed
- Zest of 2 medium oranges (about 2 tablespoons)
- 1/4 cup unsalted butter, frozen
- 2/3 cup plus 1 tablespoon buttermilk, divided
- 1 cup confectioners' sugar
- 1 tablespoon heavy whipping cream
- 3 tablespoons orange juice

GLAZE SUBSTITUTE

If you don't have heavy whipping cream on hand, you can easily swap it out for equal parts milk of your choice. Alternatively, you might choose to just use orange juice without the milk or cream for an extra-tangy glaze.

1 Preheat air fryer to 320°F.

2 In a large bowl, whisk together 2 cups flour, salt, brown sugar, and orange zest until combined.

3 Grate butter into bowl, then use a rubber spatula to combine. Add 2/3 cup buttermilk and fold until all ingredients are well combined and a soft dough forms.

4 Dust a clean work surface with remaining 2 tablespoons flour and turn dough out onto surface. Form dough into a 6" circle, about 1/2" thick. Cut into six triangles. Brush each lightly with remaining 1 tablespoon buttermilk.

5 Place scones into air fryer basket, working in batches as needed. Bake 15 minutes, flipping when 2 minutes remain. Scones should be golden brown when done, and a toothpick inserted into the center comes out clean. Let cool 5 minutes.

6 To make the glaze, whisk confectioners' sugar, heavy whipping cream, and orange juice in a small bowl until smooth. Drizzle glaze over cooled scones before serving.

PER SERVING

CALORIES: 358 | **FAT:** 9g | **SODIUM:** 630mg | **CARBOHYDRATES:** 62g | **FIBER:** 1g | **SUGAR:** 30g | **PROTEIN:** 5g

Easy Jelly Donuts

If you don't have time for donuts from scratch, biscuit donuts are a great alternative, especially in the air fryer. These donuts are golden brown and crispy on the outside while staying light and fluffy inside. Feel free to swap out the strawberry jelly for your favorite flavor instead!

Hands-on time: 10 minutes
Cook time: 14 minutes

Yields 8, 1 per serving

1 (16.3-ounce) can buttermilk biscuit dough, 8 count
1/3 cup strawberry jelly
1/4 cup salted butter, melted
1/4 cup confectioners' sugar

1 Preheat air fryer to 370°F.

2 Place each biscuit into the air fryer basket, working in batches as needed.

3 Bake 7 minutes or until golden brown, then let cool for 10 minutes.

4 Fit a piping bag with a filling nozzle and fill the bag with the jelly. Insert the nozzle into the side of each donut, pressing gently for about 2 seconds to fill each donut.

5 Brush each donut with butter. Place confectioners' sugar into a large storage bag and place donuts into the bag two at a time, shaking gently to coat them in sugar.

PER SERVING

CALORIES: 236 | FAT: 6g | SODIUM: 542mg | CARBOHYDRATES: 39g | FIBER: 1g | SUGAR: 12g | PROTEIN: 4g

Yeast Donuts

This lightened-up version is a great way to enjoy donuts without all the excess oil.

Hands-on time: 10 minutes
Cook time: 20 minutes

Yields 8, 1 per serving

1/2 cup lukewarm whole milk
3 tablespoons granulated sugar
2 teaspoons active dry yeast
1 large egg
1/4 cup salted butter, melted
2 1/4 cups plus 4 tablespoons all-purpose flour, divided
1/4 teaspoon salt
1/4 cup unsalted butter, melted
2 cups confectioners' sugar
4 tablespoons heavy whipping cream

GLAZE

Feel free to experiment with flavors for the glaze. This recipe uses a standard glaze, but you can do everything from adding spices and maple extract to even simply coating these donuts with a cinnamon-sugar mix.

1 In a medium bowl, mix milk and sugar. Gently stir in yeast and let it activate 10 minutes or until foamy.

2 In a large bowl, combine egg, salted butter, 2 1/4 cups flour, and salt. Add yeast mixture and stir until a soft dough forms.

3 Dust a clean work surface with 2 tablespoons flour and knead dough 5 minutes or until smooth and elastic.

4 Spray a large bowl with cooking spray. Place dough in bowl and cover with plastic wrap. Let rise in a warm place until almost doubled in size, about 2 hours.

5 Dust a clean work surface with remaining flour and roll dough out to 1/2" thickness.

6 Preheat air fryer to 350°F.

7 Using a 3" donut cutter, cut eight donuts and donut holes.

8 Spray donut holes and each side of donuts with cooking spray. Place donuts into air fryer basket, working in batches. Bake 6 minutes, flipping when 2 minutes remain.

9 To cook donut holes, place into air fryer basket, working in batches. Bake 4 minutes, shaking the basket halfway through cook time.

10 To make the glaze, whisk together unsalted butter, confectioners' sugar, and heavy whipping cream in a medium bowl.

11 Let donuts cool completely, then dip into glaze and place on a lined rack. Serve immediately.

PER SERVING

CALORIES: 392 | FAT: 15g | SODIUM: 138mg | CARBOHYDRATES: 58g | FIBER: 1g | SUGAR: 30g | PROTEIN: 6g

Cinnamon Chip Scones

These scones are perfect for a warm fall breakfast with coffee. The aromatic spice and cinnamon glaze in each bite is a cinnamon lover's dream. Cinnamon chips look like chocolate chips, but they're a sweetened morsel of concentrated cinnamon. They're usually found right next to the chocolate chips in the baking aisle.

Hands-on time: 10 minutes
Cook time: 30 minutes

Yields 6, 1 per serving

- 2 cups plus 2 tablespoons self-rising flour, divided
- 1/4 teaspoon salt
- 1/3 cup light brown sugar, packed
- 2 tablespoons granulated sugar
- 1/4 cup unsalted butter, frozen
- 2/3 cup whole milk
- 1/2 cup cinnamon baking chips
- 2 tablespoons heavy whipping cream, divided
- 1 cup confectioners' sugar
- 1/2 teaspoon ground cinnamon

1 Preheat air fryer to 320°F.

2 In a large bowl, whisk together 2 cups flour, salt, brown sugar, and granulated sugar until combined.

3 Grate butter into bowl, then use a rubber spatula to combine. Add milk and fold until all ingredients are well combined and a soft dough forms. Fold in cinnamon chips.

4 Dust a clean work surface with remaining 2 tablespoons flour and turn dough out onto surface. Form dough into a 6" circle, about 1/2" thick. Cut into six triangles. Brush each lightly with 1 tablespoon heavy whipping cream.

5 Place scones into air fryer basket, working in batches as needed. Bake 15 minutes, flipping when 2 minutes remain. Edges will be golden brown when done, and a toothpick inserted into the center comes out clean.

6 To make the glaze, whisk together confectioners' sugar, cinnamon, and remaining 1 tablespoon heavy whipping cream in a small bowl. Drizzle glaze over scones before serving.

PER SERVING

CALORIES: 467 | FAT: 16g | SODIUM: 658mg | CARBOHYDRATES: 73g | FIBER: 1g | SUGAR: 42g | PROTEIN: 7g

Chai-Spiced Scones

These scones taste like a chai latte, minus the cup. All the best flavors of chai tea make this a delectable fall-flavored scone. This recipe lists the ingredients for spices, but you can also find premade chai spice blends at the store that will work just as well.

Hands-on time: 15 minutes
Cook time: 30 minutes

Yields 6, 1 per serving

2 cups plus 2 tablespoons self-rising flour, divided
1/2 teaspoon salt
1/2 cup light brown sugar, packed
1/2 teaspoon ground cinnamon
1/2 teaspoon ground ginger
1/4 teaspoon ground cardamom
1/4 teaspoon ground cloves
1/4 cup unsalted butter, frozen
2/3 cup plus 2 tablespoons heavy whipping cream, divided
1/2 cup confectioners' sugar

1 Preheat air fryer to 320°F.

2 In a large bowl, whisk together 2 cups flour, salt, and brown sugar. Add cinnamon, ginger, cardamom, and cloves and stir to combine.

3 Grate butter into bowl, then use a rubber spatula to combine. Add 2/3 cup heavy whipping cream and fold until all ingredients are well combined and a soft dough forms.

4 Dust a clean work surface with remaining 2 tablespoons flour, then turn dough out onto surface. Form into a 6" circle, about 1/2" thick. Cut into six triangles. Brush each lightly with 1 tablespoon heavy whipping cream.

5 Place scones into air fryer basket, working in batches as needed. Bake 15 minutes, flipping when 2 minutes remain. Scones will be golden brown when done, and a toothpick inserted into the center comes out clean. Let cool 5 minutes.

6 To make the glaze, whisk together remaining 1 tablespoon heavy whipping cream and confectioners' sugar in a small bowl. Drizzle glaze over cooled scones before serving.

PER SERVING

CALORIES: 426 | **FAT:** 18g | **SODIUM:** 708mg | **CARBOHYDRATES:** 59g | **FIBER:** 1g | **SUGAR:** 27g | **PROTEIN:** 5g

Mini Cherry Turnovers

Mini Cherry Turnovers are perfect for breakfast or an afternoon treat. Puff pastry in the air fryer is always delicious. It's a dough best cooked quickly, and the air fryer does just that. Coarse decorating sugar makes the turnovers look extra nice. It's usually found near the sprinkles in the cake decorating aisle. If you don't have it, don't worry; it's just a finishing sprinkle. You can omit it and still enjoy these delicious pastries.

Hands-on time: 10 minutes
Cook time: 20 minutes

Yields 6, 1 per serving

1 (13.2-ounce) package
  frozen puff pastry, thawed
³/₄ cup cherry pie filling
1 large egg, whisked
1 tablespoon water
1 tablespoon coarse
  decorating sugar

ADD A GLAZE

A simple glaze takes these turnovers to the next level, and it's easier to make than you might think. After you make these treats, just whisk ¼ cup confectioners' sugar and 1 tablespoon milk, then drizzle over the cooled turnovers for an extra-sweet bite.

1 Preheat air fryer to 350°F.

2 Unroll puff pastry and place on a clean work surface. Cut sheet into six pieces by cutting it lengthwise into three large strips, then cutting each of those into two pieces.

3 Place 2 tablespoons pie filling in the center of each rectangle, then fold each over and press edges down to seal closed. Use a knife to cut three slits into top of each turnover.

4 In a small bowl, mix egg and water, then lightly brush mixture over each turnover. Sprinkle with decorating sugar.

5 Lightly spray air fryer basket with cooking spray. Place turnovers into air fryer basket, working in batches as needed. Bake 10 minutes, carefully flipping when 2 minutes remain. Turnovers will be golden brown when done. Let cool at least 10 minutes before serving.

PER SERVING

CALORIES: 403 | FAT: 23g | SODIUM: 173mg | CARBOHYDRATES: 40g | FIBER: 1g | SUGAR: 3g | PROTEIN: 6g

Lemon Poppy Seed Scones

These bright scones will start your morning right! Using zest in recipes is a great way to get a burst of lemon, and these scones use a lot. To make them even more lemony, the glaze is made from lemon juice, so there's a ton of citrus flavor in every bite.

Hands-on time: 15 minutes
Cook time: 30 minutes

Yields 8, 1 per serving

2 cups plus 2 tablespoons all-purpose flour, divided
$1/2$ cup granulated sugar
$1/4$ teaspoon salt
6 tablespoons salted butter, frozen
1 large egg
$3/4$ cup heavy whipping cream
1 teaspoon vanilla extract
2 medium lemons, zested and juiced, divided
1 teaspoon lemon extract
2 tablespoons poppy seeds
$1/2$ cup confectioners' sugar

1 Preheat air fryer to 320°F. Cut a piece of parchment to fit air fryer basket.

2 In a large bowl, whisk together 2 cups flour, granulated sugar, and salt. Grate in butter and whisk together.

3 In a medium bowl, whisk together egg, heavy whipping cream, vanilla, lemon zest and juice (reserving 2 tablespoons of juice), lemon extract, and poppy seeds.

4 Slowly add the wet ingredients to the dry ingredients, stirring until just combined.

5 Dust a clean work surface with remaining 2 tablespoons flour, then turn dough out onto surface. Form into a 6" circle and gently flatten to about $1^1/2$" thickness. Cut into eight even pieces.

6 Place into air fryer basket, working in batches as needed. Bake 15 minutes or until golden brown, flipping when 2 minutes remain. Let cool 5 minutes.

7 To make the glaze, whisk together confectioners' sugar and remaining 2 tablespoons lemon juice in a small bowl. Drizzle glaze over scones before serving.

PER SERVING

CALORIES: 363 | FAT: 17g | SODIUM: 159mg | CARBOHYDRATES: 44g | FIBER: 1g | SUGAR: 20g | PROTEIN: 5g

Strawberry Pastries

This recipe is a spin on the classic toaster pastries. It uses a mix of premade and fresh ingredients for an elevated version. Each bite is filled with strawberries and the delicious golden crust. Feel free to add sprinkles to the top or add a few drops of food coloring to the glaze to make it feel festive.

Hands-on time: 15 minutes
Cook time: 30 minutes

Yields 8, 1 per serving

1 (15-ounce) package refrigerated premade pie crust dough
1 cup strawberry jam
2 teaspoons cornstarch
5 medium strawberries, hulled and chopped
1 large egg, whisked
1/2 cup confectioners' sugar
1 tablespoon whole milk

1 Preheat air fryer to 320°F. Cut a piece of parchment to fit air fryer basket.

2 Unroll pie crust on a clean work surface and cut into six 4" × 3" rectangles. Form remaining dough into a ball and roll out to cut four additional rectangles of the same size, bringing the total to sixteen. Make two rows of eight rectangles.

3 In a small bowl, whisk together jam and cornstarch. On the bottom row of dough rectangles, place 2 tablespoons jam mixture and 1 tablespoon chopped strawberries on each piece, leaving a 1/2" border.

4 Place the top row of dough rectangles onto the filled bottoms and press edges together to seal. Use a fork around edges to crimp closed.

5 Brush pastries with egg and make a small X in the center of each using a fork. Place pastries on parchment.

6 Place parchment into air fryer basket, working in batches as needed. Bake 12 minutes, then carefully flip and cook for an additional 3 minutes or until both sides are golden brown. Let cool 10 minutes before frosting.

7 To make the frosting, whisk together confectioners' sugar and milk in a small bowl until smooth. Place 1 tablespoon on each pastry and serve.

PER SERVING

CALORIES: 386 | FAT: 13g | SODIUM: 239mg | CARBOHYDRATES: 62g | FIBER: 2g | SUGAR: 26g | PROTEIN: 3g

Raspberry and Cream Cheese Breakfast Pastries

This recipe is perfect for a special weekend breakfast. It's similar to frozen toaster pastries but with a much fresher flavor. The flaky golden layers are a perfect complement to the tangy raspberry flavor. You can swap the preserves out for whatever you have on hand or your favorite flavor, such as strawberry or cherry.

Hands-on time: 15 minutes
Cook time: 30 minutes

Yields 4, 1 per serving

1 (13.2-ounce) package frozen puff pastry, thawed
2 ounces cream cheese, softened
4 tablespoons raspberry preserves
1 teaspoon cornstarch
1 large egg, whisked
1 tablespoon whole milk
$1/2$ cup confectioners' sugar

1 Preheat air fryer to 350°F.

2 Cut puff pastry into eight rectangles. Spread $1/2$ ounce cream cheese on each of four rectangles.

3 In a small bowl, mix preserves and cornstarch. Place 1 tablespoon jam on top of cream cheese.

4 Top each with 1 plain puff pastry piece and press edges together to seal closed. Brush pastry tops with egg.

5 Place pastries into air fryer basket. Bake 15 minutes, flipping when 5 minutes remain. Both sides should be golden brown when done. Let cool 5 minutes.

6 To make the glaze, whisk together milk and confectioners' sugar in a small bowl. Drizzle glaze over each pastry before serving.

PER SERVING

CALORIES: 690 | FAT: 39g | SODIUM: 310mg | CARBOHYDRATES: 70g | FIBER: 2g | SUGAR: 23g | PROTEIN: 9g

Cream Cheese Danish

This classic recipe is tasty and quick. If you're short on time in the mornings, in just 20 minutes you can enjoy a creamy, crispy pastry for breakfast. You can keep it simple or add your own twist by drizzling with chocolate hazelnut spread or your favorite berries.

Hands-on time: 10 minutes
Cook time: 10 minutes

Yields 4, 1 per serving

4 ounces cream cheese, softened
4 tablespoons granulated sugar
2 teaspoons lemon juice
1 (13.2-ounce) package frozen puff pastry, thawed

TOP IT WITH FRUIT

This Danish is delicious just the way it is. But for an extra layer of flavor, try adding a tablespoon of cherry pie filling on top or your favorite fruit preserves.

1   Preheat air fryer to 350°F.

2   In a medium bowl, whisk together cream cheese, sugar, and lemon juice.

3   Place puff pastry on a clean work surface and cut into four even pieces. Cut each portion into three strips lengthwise.

4   Roll the first pastry strip into a spiral and flatten. Hold the second pastry strip with an end in each hand. Twist four times then place on top of the spiral, gently pressing pieces together. Repeat with the third pastry strip, and place it around the other two pieces. Repeat process for remaining three pieces of puff pastry.

5   Place 1 tablespoon cream cheese mixture in the center of each Danish.

6   Place Danish into air fryer basket, working in batches as needed. Bake 10 minutes or until golden brown. Serve warm.

PER SERVING

CALORIES: 660 | FAT: 42g | SODIUM: 336mg | CARBOHYDRATES: 56g | FIBER: 1g | SUGAR: 14g | PROTEIN: 9g

Triple-Berry Danish

The natural tart taste and sweetness of fresh fruit can't be beat. This recipe is perfect for those who love fruit and cheesecake together. The homemade sauce comes together on the stove in just 10 minutes but is the star of this yummy breakfast pastry.

Hands-on time: 20 minutes
Cook time: 34 minutes

Yields 6, 1 per serving

- 1/2 cup strawberries, hulled and chopped
- 1/4 cup blueberries
- 1/4 cup raspberries
- 1/3 cup plus 2 tablespoons granulated sugar, divided
- 1 tablespoon cornstarch
- 2 tablespoons water
- 6 tablespoons cream cheese, softened
- 2 teaspoons lemon juice
- 1 (13.2-ounce) package frozen puff pastry, thawed

1 In a small saucepan over medium heat, add strawberries, blueberries, raspberries, and 1/3 cup sugar. Cook 5 minutes, stirring frequently until berries break down.

2 In a small bowl, whisk together cornstarch and water. Pour mixture into pan with berries and stir frequently until mixture begins to thicken and resemble a thick jam, about 5 minutes. Remove from heat and let cool 5 minutes.

3 Preheat air fryer to 350°F. Cut a piece of parchment to fit air fryer basket.

4 In a medium bowl, mix remaining 2 tablespoons sugar, cream cheese, and lemon juice until smooth.

5 Unroll puff pastry on a clean work surface and slice into six pieces.

6 Place 1 tablespoon cream cheese mixture in the center of each puff pastry piece, then top with 1 1/2 tablespoons berry sauce.

7 Fold puff pastry edges toward the center, leaving about 1" in the center exposed.

8 Place Danish on parchment and place parchment into air fryer basket, working in batches as needed. Bake 12 minutes or until edges are golden brown. Let cool 5 minutes before serving.

PER SERVING

CALORIES: 467 | FAT: 27g | SODIUM: 208mg | CARBOHYDRATES: 48g | FIBER: 2g | SUGAR: 18g | PROTEIN: 6g

Raspberry and Cream Cheese Braid

This recipe is a great way to use older raspberries that are beginning to soften. And it's also great if you're short on time, because this dish requires no fuss and comes together quickly. Its rich and sweet filling will be a hit among all ages.

Hands-on time: 15 minutes
Cook time: 12 minutes

Serves 6

1 (13.2-ounce) package frozen puff pastry, thawed
4 ounces cream cheese, softened
1/3 cup granulated sugar
1/2 teaspoon lemon juice
2 cups fresh raspberries
1 large egg
1 tablespoon water

1 Preheat air fryer to 320°F.

2 Unroll puff pastry and place vertically on a clean work surface.

3 In a medium bowl, mix cream cheese, sugar, and lemon juice until smooth.

4 Spread cream cheese mixture in the center of puff pastry, about 2" wide down the width of the dough.

5 Place raspberries on top of cream cheese mixture.

6 Cut long sides of puff pastry into 2" strips, leaving the center with filling intact. Close braid by placing the top left strip into the center, on top of filling, and crossing the top-right strip over, slightly overlapping. Continue with the remaining strips until filling is enclosed.

7 In a small bowl, whisk together egg and water. Gently brush mixture over braid.

8 Place braid into air fryer basket. Bake 12 minutes or until top and sides are golden brown and let cool for 5 minutes. Serve warm.

PER SERVING

CALORIES: 484 | FAT: 29g | SODIUM: 236mg | CARBOHYDRATES: 45g | FIBER: 4g | SUGAR: 14g | PROTEIN: 7g

Lemon Biscuit Danish

Refrigerated biscuits can be a lifesaver when it seems everyone is getting hangry. This Danish is bursting with yummy lemon flavor and will be ready in just minutes! For this recipe you'll need to buy jumbo biscuits to support the filling. If you already have the smaller ones, just halve the filling ingredients or use two cans of biscuits.

Hands-on time: 10 minutes
Cook time: 16 minutes

Yields 16, 2 per serving

1 (16-ounce) can jumbo flaky refrigerated biscuits, 8 count
4 ounces cream cheese, softened
1/4 cup granulated sugar
1/2 teaspoon vanilla extract
8 teaspoons lemon curd
1/2 cup confectioners' sugar
1 tablespoon whole milk

1 Preheat air fryer to 350°F. Cut a piece of parchment to fit air fryer basket.

2 Carefully split each biscuit lengthwise to make two biscuits. Gently flatten each into 1/4" thickness.

3 In a medium bowl, stir cream cheese, sugar, and vanilla until well combined.

4 Place 1/2 tablespoon cream cheese mixture in the center of each biscuit, then place 1/2 teaspoon lemon curd on top of cream cheese. Place Danish on parchment.

5 Place parchment into air fryer basket, working in batches as needed. Bake 8 minutes or until biscuits are golden brown. Let cool for 5 minutes.

6 To make the glaze, whisk together confectioners' sugar and milk in a small bowl. Drizzle glaze over Danish before serving.

PER SERVING

CALORIES: 297 | FAT: 8g | SODIUM: 661mg | CARBOHYDRATES: 43g | FIBER: 1g | SUGAR: 22g | PROTEIN: 5g

Double Chocolate Chip Scones

Double chocolate might not be the first scone flavor that comes to mind, but it's about to become your favorite. All the best parts of a double chocolate chip cookie and the sweet, buttery flavor of a biscuit combine here to give you the best dessert scone you've tasted. These scones are filled with rich flavor and gooey chocolate chips that will make you keep coming back for more.

Hands-on time: 10 minutes
Cook time: 30 minutes

Yields 8, 1 per serving

1 cup buttermilk
1 large egg
1 teaspoon vanilla extract
1³/₄ cups plus 2 tablespoons all-purpose flour, divided
¹/₄ cup unsweetened cocoa powder
¹/₂ cup light brown sugar, packed
¹/₂ teaspoon baking powder
¹/₄ teaspoon salt
6 tablespoons unsalted butter, frozen
¹/₂ cup semisweet chocolate chips

1 Preheat air fryer to 320°F. Cut a piece of parchment to fit air fryer basket.

2 In a small bowl, whisk together buttermilk, egg, and vanilla until combined.

3 In a large bowl, whisk together 1³/₄ cups flour, cocoa powder, brown sugar, baking powder, and salt until combined.

4 Grate butter into flour mixture, then use a wooden spoon to evenly distribute. Pour buttermilk mixture into flour mixture and stir until all ingredients are well combined and a soft dough forms. Fold in chocolate chips.

5 Dust a clean work surface with remaining 2 tablespoons flour and turn dough out onto surface. Knead dough a couple of times and gently form into a 6" circle. Cut into eight triangles and place on parchment, leaving at least a 2" space between each.

6 Place parchment into air fryer basket, working in batches as needed.

7 Bake 15 minutes or until edges are crispy and a toothpick inserted into the center of scones comes out clean. Let cool at least 10 minutes before serving.

PER SERVING

CALORIES: 318 | FAT: 13g | SODIUM: 151mg | CARBOHYDRATES: 45g | FIBER: 2g | SUGAR: 21g | PROTEIN: 6g

Chocolate-Dipped Cream Puffs

Don't let pastry dough scare you. These cream puffs are easier than you think. If you're new to baking, you can give this recipe a try with confidence. To make things simple, the filling is instant pudding. These cream puffs are like delicious mini pillows topped with a creamy, decadent topping.

Hands-on time: 15 minutes
Cook time: 29 minutes

Yields 12, 1 per serving

1 (3.4-ounce) box instant vanilla pudding
1 cup whole milk
1/2 cup salted butter
3/4 cup water
1 cup all-purpose flour
1/4 teaspoon salt
3 large eggs
1 large egg yolk
1/2 cup semisweet chocolate chips
2 tablespoons heavy whipping cream

1 In a medium bowl, whisk together pudding and milk. Place in refrigerator to cool until ready to use.

2 In a small saucepan over medium heat, melt butter and water, bringing to a boil. Add flour and salt, then turn off heat. Stir vigorously until a soft, smooth ball of dough forms. Place dough in a large bowl and let cool 5 minutes.

3 Stir in eggs and egg yolk, one at a time, until fully incorporated.

4 Preheat air fryer to 320°F. Cut a piece of parchment to fit air fryer basket.

5 Drop 2 tablespoonfuls of dough on parchment to form a puff. Repeat with remaining dough, leaving at least a 2" space between each. Makes 12 puffs.

6 Place parchment into air fryer basket, working in batches. Bake 12 minutes or until golden brown. Let cool 20 minutes.

7 Cut puffs in half and fill with pudding using a piping bag with filling tip.

8 In a microwave-safe bowl, melt chocolate chips and heavy whipping cream 30 seconds. Stir until completely smooth, then dip the top of each cream puff in chocolate. Let sit 15 minutes before serving.

PER SERVING

CALORIES: 215 | FAT: 12g | SODIUM: 189mg | CARBOHYDRATES: 21g | FIBER: 1g | SUGAR: 12g | PROTEIN: 4g

Chocolate Hazelnut Braids

This decadent recipe is a crowd-pleaser, popular among kids and adults alike. Each bite is filled with melt-in-your-mouth flavors. This is a great last-minute dessert you can quickly whip up for any occasion. It's sure to impress.

Hands-on time: 15 minutes
Cook time: 24 minutes

Serves 6

1 (17.3-ounce) package frozen puff pastry, thawed
1 cup chocolate hazelnut spread
1 large egg, whisked
2 tablespoons confectioners' sugar

1 Preheat air fryer to 350°F.

2 Unroll puff pastry on a clean work surface and spread chocolate hazelnut spread over entire puff pastry.

3 Roll puff pastry into a log, beginning with a short side. Cut the log into two equal pieces.

4 Press edges of one log together at the non-cut end. Leaving a 1" border, use a knife to slice into three equal parts down the length of the log. Braid the pieces by overlapping the middle piece over the front and behind the left piece. Repeat to the end of puff pastry and press together to seal. Repeat process with remaining log.

5 Brush braids with egg.

6 Place braids into air fryer basket, working in batches as needed. Bake 12 minutes or until braids are golden brown on both sides. Let cool 10 minutes, then dust with confectioners' sugar before serving.

PER SERVING

CALORIES: 739 | FAT: 44g | SODIUM: 235mg | CARBOHYDRATES: 70g | FIBER: 4g | SUGAR: 30g | PROTEIN: 10g

Stuffed Croissant French Toast

Breakfast just got more delicious! This recipe comes together fast but tastes like you spent all morning in the kitchen. The key is finding the best fluffy, fresh croissants at the store. The fresher they are, the better the whole recipe will be.

Hands-on time: 10 minutes
Cook time: 6 minutes

Yields 4, 1 per serving

- 4 medium-sized croissants
- 2 ounces cream cheese, softened
- 1/4 cup plus 3 tablespoons confectioners' sugar, divided
- 4 medium strawberries, hulled and sliced
- 1 large egg
- 2 tablespoons heavy whipping cream
- 1 tablespoon granulated sugar
- 1/2 teaspoon ground cinnamon

CUSTOMIZE IT

If you're hosting or attending a brunch and want to really impress everyone, consider some additional toppings. You can add some flair to this recipe by adding a drizzle of chocolate over the top, or choose to add sliced fresh fruit and whipped cream. Or all three!

1 Preheat air fryer to 375°F.

2 On one side of each croissant, cut a slit about 4" long to create a pocket.

3 In a medium bowl, combine cream cheese and 1/4 cup confectioners' sugar until smooth. Distribute mixture evenly among croissants, gently spooning it into the pocket of each croissant in a smooth layer. Layer strawberries on top of cream cheese in each croissant and press to close the pocket.

4 In a large bowl, whisk together egg, heavy whipping cream, granulated sugar, and cinnamon.

5 Press both sides of each croissant into mixture, as you would with French toast, letting the excess drip off.

6 Place croissants into air fryer basket, working in batches as needed. Bake 6 minutes, flipping when 2 minutes remain. Croissants will be dark golden brown when done. Let cool 5 minutes. Dust with remaining 3 tablespoons confectioners' sugar before serving.

PER SERVING

CALORIES: 389 | FAT: 18g | SODIUM: 338mg | CARBOHYDRATES: 44g | FIBER: 2g | SUGAR: 23g | PROTEIN: 7g

Apple-Stuffed Cinnamon Rolls

This yummy recipe takes canned cinnamon rolls and adds a twist. Making cinnamon rolls from scratch can be time-consuming, and sometimes cravings hit at inconvenient times. While canned cinnamon rolls are delicious, adding a few extra ingredients can really step things up and make them even better. These fresh additions brighten up this whole dish, and the recipe still takes only minimal effort and time.

Hands-on time: 15 minutes
Cook time: 12 minutes

Yields 6, 1 per serving

1 large Honeycrisp apple, peeled, cored, and chopped
2 tablespoons light brown sugar, packed
2 teaspoons lemon juice
1 (12.4-ounce) can refrigerated cinnamon rolls

1 Preheat air fryer to 320°F. Cut a piece of parchment to fit air fryer basket.

2 In a medium bowl, toss apple, brown sugar, and lemon juice until well combined.

3 Remove cinnamon rolls from the can and carefully unroll each cinnamon roll.

4 Place 2 tablespoons apple mixture on each dough piece, then roll up, gently pressing each seam closed. Place on parchment.

5 Place parchment into air fryer basket. Bake 12 minutes or until golden brown. Let cool 10 minutes before icing and serving.

CUSTOMIZE IT

Often canned cinnamon rolls come with premade frosting. Use this as a base, and if you'd like a little more flavor in yours, you can add ½ teaspoon ground cinnamon or even 1 tablespoon orange zest. Just mix it in right before serving.

PER SERVING

CALORIES: 161 | **FAT:** 1g | **SODIUM:** 296mg | **CARBOHYDRATES:** 29g | **FIBER:** 1g | **SUGAR:** 16g | **PROTEIN:** 2g

Cinnamon-Sugar Crescent Rolls

These treats couldn't be easier to make, and their delicious flavor will make them a regular in your baking rotation. Think of them as lazy cinnamon rolls—full of delicious flavor, and, thanks to your air fryer, they take a fraction of the cook time!

Hands-on time: 5 minutes
Cook time: 5 minutes

Yields 8, 1 per serving

1 (8-ounce) can roll crescent dough, 8 count
$1/3$ cup granulated sugar
1 tablespoon ground cinnamon
2 tablespoons salted butter, melted

1 Preheat air fryer to 400°F.

2 Place dough on a clean work surface and separate each crescent roll.

3 In a small bowl, mix sugar and cinnamon. Sprinkle mixture on each crescent roll dough piece.

4 Starting with the widest end, roll up crescent rolls. Brush each crescent roll with butter.

5 Place crescent rolls into air fryer basket. Bake 5 minutes, flipping after 3 minutes. Crescent rolls will be golden brown when done. Serve warm.

PER SERVING

CALORIES: 161 | FAT: 8g | SODIUM: 235mg | CARBOHYDRATES: 21g | FIBER: 1g | SUGAR: 11g | PROTEIN: 2g

Caramel Apple Dumplings

Nothing says "cozy fall night" like warm spiced apples. This recipe makes an elegant dessert easy. The flaky pastry makes the most delicious house for the sweet apples. Honeycrisp is suggested for this recipe because of the balance of sweet and tartness, but any apples you have on hand can work, especially Fuji or Gala apples.

Hands-on time: 15 minutes
Cook time: 12 minutes

Yields 4, 1 per serving

- 1 (13.2-ounce) package frozen puff pastry, thawed
- 2 tablespoons light brown sugar, packed
- 2 medium Honeycrisp apples, cored and cut into 1/4" slices
- 1 teaspoon ground cinnamon
- 1/2 teaspoon cornstarch
- 1 large egg, whisked
- 1 tablespoon coarse sparkling sugar
- 4 tablespoons caramel sauce

SERVING IDEAS

Ready to take this treat to the next level? Try adding a spoonful of whipped cream or a scoop of vanilla ice cream to this dish. The warm dumpling combined with the cool topping will add a delicious sense of comfort.

1 Preheat air fryer to 350°F.

2 Unroll puff pastry on a clean work surface and cut into four equal pieces. Place 1/2 tablespoon brown sugar on each piece.

3 In a medium bowl, toss apples, cinnamon, and cornstarch until all pieces are coated.

4 Distribute the coated apples evenly among puff pastry pieces, placing the apples in the center of each piece and stacking and overlapping as needed to keep the apples in a pile.

5 Fold opposing corners of puff pastry toward the center, pinching at the top. Pinch all meeting edges together to completely seal closed. Brush egg over each dumpling and sprinkle with sparkling sugar.

6 Place dumplings into air fryer basket. Bake 12 minutes or until golden brown. Let cool 15 minutes, then drizzle with caramel sauce. Serve warm.

PER SERVING

CALORIES: 673 | FAT: 35g | SODIUM: 324mg | CARBOHYDRATES: 78g | FIBER: 4g | SUGAR: 19g | PROTEIN: 9g

Peach Crescent Roll-Ups

If you love peaches, you'll love these easy bites. They're golden brown and crusty with a soft, delicious fruit-filled center. This recipe uses full dough sheets, but if you can't find those, feel free to use regular crescent roll dough and press the seams together before you begin.

Hands-on time: 10 minutes
Cook time: 8 minutes

Yields 12, 1 per serving

2 (8-ounce) cans crescent roll dough
1 (15-ounce) can peach pie filling
1/4 cup light brown sugar, packed
1 tablespoon ground cinnamon, divided
4 tablespoons salted butter, melted
1/4 cup granulated sugar

1 Preheat air fryer to 350°F.

2 Unroll dough on a clean work surface and cut into twelve rectangles, six per sheet.

3 In a medium bowl, mix pie filling, brown sugar, and 1 teaspoon cinnamon. Place 3 tablespoons mixture on the lower third of each dough piece.

4 Carefully roll up each dough piece, starting at the side closest to peach mixture. Brush each roll with butter.

5 In a small bowl, mix remaining 2 teaspoons cinnamon and granulated sugar. Sprinkle each side of rolls with mixture.

6 Place rolls into air fryer basket, working in batches as needed. Bake 8 minutes, flipping after 5 minutes to evenly brown both sides. Transfer to a serving tray and let cool 10 minutes before serving.

PER SERVING

CALORIES: 251 | FAT: 10g | SODIUM: 324mg | CARBOHYDRATES: 37g | FIBER: 0g | SUGAR: 23g | PROTEIN: 3g

Peaches and Cream Fritters

Traditionally, fritters are deep-fried in oil to get a golden brown exterior. This lighter version has fewer calories than the deep-fried version but all the same crunch. These drop biscuit–style fritters pack a punch of deliciousness in every bite. To make sure your fritters get the max crunch, don't worry about shaping each spoonful. Any pieces of dough that stick up will turn into golden bites that will likely be your favorites.

Hands-on time: 10 minutes
Cook time: 16 minutes

Yields 16, 2 per serving

2 cups plus 2 tablespoons self-rising flour, divided
1/4 teaspoon salt
1/2 teaspoon ground cinnamon
1/4 cup granulated sugar
1/4 cup salted butter, frozen
1 (15-ounce) can peaches, drained and chopped
2/3 cup whole milk
1/4 cup confectioners' sugar
1 tablespoon heavy whipping cream

1 Preheat air fryer to 350°F. Cut a piece of parchment to fit air fryer basket.

2 In a large bowl, whisk together 2 cups flour, salt, cinnamon, and granulated sugar until well combined.

3 Grate butter and add to the bowl, then stir in peaches and milk until a soft dough forms.

4 Scoop dough by the tablespoon and place on parchment.

5 Place parchment into air fryer basket, working in batches as needed. Bake 8 minutes or until golden brown.

6 To make the glaze, whisk confectioners' sugar and heavy whipping cream in a small bowl until smooth. Let fritters cool at least 15 minutes, then drizzle with glaze before serving.

PER SERVING

CALORIES: 125 | FAT: 3g | SODIUM: 251mg | CARBOHYDRATES: 21g | FIBER: 1g | SUGAR: 9g | PROTEIN: 2g

4

Cookies

Of course cookies deserve their own chapter! Whether you're whipping up a batch by yourself or spending precious family time together in the kitchen, your air fryer can help you achieve amazing, fresh-baked goodies that will have you reaching for an ice-cold glass of milk.

Cookies don't have to be tricky just because you're using a smaller surface, like your air fryer basket. Just remember to cook in batches as necessary, or modify the cookie shapes and sizes to make more or fewer than what the recipe calls for. For example, you could make a dozen cookies, but nobody would be upset that you saved time by making one scrumptious giant cookie cake.

With recipes from Brown Butter Chocolate Chip Cookies to Coconut Macaroons, this chapter has something for everyone.

Inside-Out Chocolate Chip Cookies

These delicious cookies are a twist on a well-loved classic. This recipe turns traditional chocolate chip cookies inside out by using a chocolate dough and white chocolate chips. Perfectly indulgent and rich with flavor, these soft and gooey chocolate cookies will become your new go-to.

Hands-on time: 15 minutes
Cook time: 30 minutes

Yields 12, 1 per serving

- ½ cup salted butter, melted
- ½ cup light brown sugar, packed
- ¼ cup granulated sugar
- 1 large egg
- 1 teaspoon vanilla extract
- 1 cup all-purpose flour
- ¼ cup unsweetened cocoa powder
- 1 teaspoon baking powder
- ½ cup white chocolate chips

1 In a large bowl, use an electric hand mixer to beat butter, brown sugar, and granulated sugar until creamy, about 1 minute. Gently mix in egg and vanilla until just combined.

2 In a separate large bowl, mix flour, cocoa powder, and baking powder until well combined.

3 Slowly mix the wet ingredients into the dry ingredients until just combined.

4 Gently fold in white chocolate chips. Chill dough in refrigerator 10 minutes.

5 Preheat air fryer to 350°F. Cut a piece of parchment to fit air fryer basket.

6 Scoop about 2 tablespoons dough into a ball and set on parchment. Repeat with remaining dough, leaving 2" of space in between.

7 Place parchment into air fryer basket, working in batches as needed. Bake 10 minutes or until firm on bottom and edges. Transfer to a wire rack to cool. Serve warm.

PER SERVING

CALORIES: 205 | FAT: 10g | SODIUM: 116mg | CARBOHYDRATES: 27g | FIBER: 1g | SUGAR: 17g | PROTEIN: 2g

Brownie Batter Cookies

These cookies taste just like brownies but cook in way less time! The edges are soft and cake-like, while the insides are gooey and fudgy. They're the best of both worlds. If you love extra-chocolaty cookies, this recipe is a must try.

Hands-on time: 11 minutes
Cook time: 24 minutes

Yields 12, 1 per serving

1 cup semisweet chocolate chips
¼ cup salted butter, cubed
⅓ cup light brown sugar, packed
¼ cup all-purpose flour
1 teaspoon vanilla extract
1 large egg, beaten

1 Preheat air fryer to 375°F and cut a piece of parchment to fit air fryer basket.

2 In a medium microwave-safe bowl, melt chocolate chips and butter in 30-second increments, about 1 minute total. Stir between each heating.

3 Stir in brown sugar, flour, and vanilla until fully combined. Stir in egg until a smooth dough forms.

4 Drop heaping tablespoonfuls of dough onto parchment, leaving 2" of space in between.

5 Place parchment into air fryer basket. Bake 8 minutes or until cookies are puffy. As they cool, they will settle into a chewy, fudgy, brownie-like texture. Serve warm.

PER SERVING

CALORIES: 146 | FAT: 8g | SODIUM: 39mg | CARBOHYDRATES: 18g | FIBER: 1g | SUGAR: 14g | PROTEIN: 1g

Brown Butter Chocolate Chip Cookies

These cookies require stove cook time, but don't let that deter you. Making brown butter is not only easy, but it also makes your cookies taste even more delicious. It adds a layer of nutty, almost caramel-like flavor. Once the dough is made, these cookies bake quickly. Your taste buds will definitely be thanking you for the extra time spent on this recipe.

Hands-on time: 20 minutes
Cook time: 39 minutes

Yields 12, 1 per serving

½ cup salted butter
1 teaspoon vanilla extract
1 cup light brown sugar, packed
1 large egg
2 cups all-purpose flour
2 teaspoons baking powder
1 cup semisweet chocolate chips

BROWNED BUTTER

If you don't want to use browned butter, that's fine. You can feel free to just skip that step and use softened butter in its place. The taste will be less caramel-like, but the consistency will still be soft and gooey.

1 In a small saucepan over medium heat, add butter. Use a rubber spatula to stir about 5 minutes or until butter begins to turn golden brown, becomes fragrant, and starts to foam. Pour into a medium bowl and let cool 5 minutes.

2 Preheat air fryer to 300°F. Cut a piece of parchment to fit air fryer basket.

3 Add vanilla and brown sugar to bowl with butter and mix. Stir in egg.

4 In a large bowl, mix flour and baking powder.

5 Slowly incorporate the wet ingredients into the dry ingredients until well combined. Fold in chocolate chips.

6 Scoop about 2 tablespoons dough, roll into a ball, then gently flatten into a ½"-thick disc. Place on parchment. Repeat with remaining dough, leaving 2" of space in between.

7 Place parchment into air fryer basket, working in batches as needed. Bake 8 minutes or until bottom and edges are golden brown. Transfer to a wire rack to cool. Serve warm.

PER SERVING

CALORIES: 293 | FAT: 12g | SODIUM: 155mg | CARBOHYDRATES: 44g | FIBER: 1g | SUGAR: 26g | PROTEIN: 3g

Wedding Cookies

These are similar to what you might think of as snowball cookies. They are yummy!

Hands-on time: 10 minutes
Cook time: 48 minutes

Yields 12, 1 per serving

1 cup all-purpose flour
1¹/₃ cups confectioners' sugar, divided
8 tablespoons salted butter, softened
1 cup pecans, finely chopped
1 teaspoon vanilla extract

1 Preheat air fryer to 320°F and cut a piece of parchment to fit the air fryer basket.

2 In a medium bowl, mix flour, ¹/₃ cup confectioners' sugar, butter, pecans, and vanilla.

3 Scoop about 2 tablespoons dough, roll into a ball, and place into air fryer basket. Repeat with remaining dough, leaving 2" of space in between. Bake 12 minutes or until golden brown, working in batches as needed. Transfer to a wire rack and let cool 5 minutes.

4 Place remaining 1 cup confectioners' sugar in a shallow bowl. Roll each cookie to coat with confectioners' sugar. Serve warm.

PER SERVING

CALORIES: 185 | **FAT:** 13g | **SODIUM:** 61mg | **CARBOHYDRATES:** 15g | **FIBER:** 1g | **SUGAR:** 6g | **PROTEIN:** 2g

Lemon Crinkle Cookies

Cake mix cookies are a great baking hack. They're full of flavor and come together in no time.

Hands-on time: 10 minutes
Cook time: 10 minutes

Yields 12, 1 per serving

1 (15.25-ounce) box lemon cake mix
2 teaspoons baking powder
¹/₃ cup salted butter, melted
1 large egg
¹/₂ cup confectioners' sugar

1 Preheat air fryer to 320°F.

2 In a large bowl, stir cake mix, baking powder, butter, and egg until a dough forms.

3 Scoop about 2 tablespoons dough and roll into a ball. Repeat with remaining dough.

4 Place confectioners' sugar on a plate. Roll each ball in confectioners' sugar, then gently flatten into a disc about ¹/₄" thick.

5 Place cookies into air fryer basket, working in batches. Bake 10 minutes or until edges are firm and the center is set. Serve warm.

PER SERVING

CALORIES: 201 | **FAT:** 6g | **SODIUM:** 395mg | **CARBOHYDRATES:** 35g | **FIBER:** 0g | **SUGAR:** 20g | **PROTEIN:** 2g

Meringues

Sometimes turning on the oven for hours feels like too much of a time commitment, even for meringues. This is where the air fryer comes in, as it heats up and sustains lower temperatures just like the oven, but it requires much less energy and time to do so. These Meringues take about a quarter of the time as some traditional recipes.

Hands-on time: 5 minutes
Cook time: 60 minutes

Yields 6, 1 per serving

2 large egg whites
1/4 teaspoon vanilla extract
1/8 teaspoon cream of tartar
1/2 cup plus 2 tablespoons granulated sugar

AIR FRYER SETTINGS

Some air fryers allow you to freely access all temperatures at the turn of the dial. With others, you may have to preselect a setting such as Dehydrate to access a wider temperature range. If you're unsure how to get down to 200°F, refer to your instruction manual.

1 Preheat air fryer to 200°F. Cut a piece of parchment to fit air fryer basket.

2 In a large bowl, use an electric hand mixer to beat egg whites, vanilla, and cream of tartar until stiff peaks form, about 4 minutes.

3 Add sugar, 1 tablespoon at a time, until glossy.

4 Spoon mixture into a piping bag fitted with a star tip. Swirl into six cookies on parchment.

5 Place parchment into air fryer basket. Bake 30 minutes, working in batches as needed. Transfer to a wire rack and let cool completely, about 15 minutes before serving.

PER SERVING

CALORIES: 86 | FAT: 0g | SODIUM: 18mg | CARBOHYDRATES: 21g | FIBER: 0g | SUGAR: 21g | PROTEIN: 1g

Sugar Cookies

Sugar cookies are a staple. They are perfect for dessert any time and are a winner for all special occasions. These Sugar Cookies are extra special because the air fryer gives the sugar just a hint of caramelization, adding a whole new flavor.

Hands-on time: 10 minutes
Cook time: 30 minutes

Yields 12, 1 per serving

1/2 cup unsalted butter, softened
1 cup plus 3 tablespoons granulated sugar, divided
1 teaspoon vanilla extract
1/2 teaspoon salt
1/2 teaspoon baking powder
1/2 teaspoon cream of tartar
1 cup all-purpose flour

1 Preheat air fryer to 325°F. Cut a piece of parchment to fit air fryer basket.

2 In a large bowl, use an electric hand mixer to beat butter and 1 cup sugar until fluffy, about 2 minutes.

3 Add vanilla and stir until combined.

4 In a small bowl, mix salt, baking powder, cream of tartar, and flour until well combined.

5 Slowly add flour mixture into butter mixture, stirring until just combined.

6 Scoop about 2 tablespoons dough, roll into a ball, then gently flatten into a disc about 1/2" thick and place on parchment. Repeat with remaining dough, leaving 2" of space between cookies. Sprinkle remaining 3 table-spoons sugar over tops of cookies.

7 Place parchment into air fryer basket, work-ing in batches as needed. Bake 10 minutes or until edges are golden brown. Transfer to a wire rack to cool. Serve warm.

PER SERVING

CALORIES: 183 | FAT: 7g | SODIUM: 118mg | CARBOHYDRATES: 28g | FIBER: 0g | SUGAR: 20g | PROTEIN: 1g

Snickerdoodles

What makes Snickerdoodles stand out is being rolled in cinnamon-sugar after they're done baking. The cookie dough is a bit less sweet than others, but the yummy outer layer makes up for it. These soft cookies have just a bit of crunch on the bottom.

Hands-on time: 10 minutes
Cook time: 30 minutes

Yields 12, 1 per serving

- 1/2 cup salted butter, softened
- 1 1/2 cups granulated sugar, divided
- 1 teaspoon vanilla extract
- 1/2 teaspoon baking powder
- 1 teaspoon cream of tartar
- 1 cup all-purpose flour
- 1 tablespoon ground cinnamon

1 Preheat air fryer to 325°F.

2 In a large bowl, use an electric hand mixer to beat butter and 1 cup sugar until fluffy, about 2 minutes. Add vanilla and stir to combine.

3 In a small bowl, mix baking powder, cream of tartar, and flour until combined. Slowly add the dry ingredients to the wet ingredients, mixing until just combined.

4 Scoop about 2 tablespoons dough and gently flatten into a disc about 1/2" thick. Repeat with remaining dough.

5 Place dough into air fryer basket, leaving at least 1 1/2" between each cookie, working in batches as needed. Bake 10 minutes or until golden brown.

6 In a shallow bowl, mix remaining 1/2 cup sugar and cinnamon. Press each cookie into mixture while still warm to coat. Transfer to a wire rack to cool. Serve warm.

PER SERVING

CALORIES: 205 | FAT: 7g | SODIUM: 81mg | CARBOHYDRATES: 34g | FIBER: 1g | SUGAR: 25g | PROTEIN: 1g

Peanut Butter Cookies

These ultra-soft cookies are comfort treats at their best. This recipe uses oil, unlike most of the cookie recipes in this book. Using oil gives these cookies a much denser, cake-like texture, which is exactly what you want. If you absolutely need to swap, just use equal amounts of melted butter, but keep in mind, the cookies won't be as dense and chewy.

Hands-on time: 15 minutes
Cook time: 60 minutes

Yields 20, 1 per serving

$1/2$ cup vegetable oil
$1^1/_4$ cups peanut butter
$3/_4$ cup light brown sugar, packed
$1/_4$ cup plus 2 tablespoons granulated sugar, divided
1 large egg
1 teaspoon vanilla extract
$1^1/_2$ cups all-purpose flour
$1/_2$ teaspoon baking powder
$1/_2$ teaspoon baking soda
$1/_4$ teaspoon salt

ADD SOME CRUNCH

If you like a little crunch in your peanut butter cookies, you can use chunky peanut butter! Or add $1/_3$ cup finely chopped unsalted peanuts to the recipe. Either way, you'll get the texture you're looking for.

1 Preheat air fryer to 325°F.

2 In a large bowl, stir oil and peanut butter. Add brown sugar and $1/_4$ cup granulated sugar and mix until well combined. Stir in egg and vanilla.

3 In a medium bowl, mix flour, baking powder, baking soda, and salt until combined.

4 Add half of the dry ingredients to the wet ingredients and mix until combined, then add the remaining dry ingredients and mix until combined.

5 Scoop about 2 tablespoons dough, roll into a ball, then gently flatten into a disc about $1/_2$" thick. Repeat with remaining dough.

6 Using a fork, press a crisscross pattern into each cookie, then sprinkle with remaining 2 tablespoons granulated sugar.

7 Place cookies into air fryer basket, working in batches as needed. Bake 12 minutes or until edges begin to lightly brown. Let cool 10 minutes before serving.

PER SERVING

CALORIES: 230 | FAT: 13g | SODIUM: 147mg | CARBOHYDRATES: 23g | FIBER: 1g | SUGAR: 14g | PROTEIN: 5g

Butter Pecan Cookies

These cookies are the perfect treat anytime. They melt in your mouth with a delicious buttery flavor that is complemented by a touch of salt from the nuts. If you're a fan of shortbread cookies, you'll love this classic flavor combination.

Hands-on time: 10 minutes
Cook time: 8 minutes

Yields 12, 1 per serving

- ½ cup salted butter, softened
- ¼ cup granulated sugar
- ½ cup light brown sugar, packed
- 1 large egg
- 1 large egg yolk
- 1 teaspoon vanilla extract
- 1 cup all-purpose flour
- 1 tablespoon cornstarch
- 1 teaspoon baking powder
- ½ teaspoon salt
- 1 cup pecans, chopped

1. In a large bowl, use an electric hand mixer to beat butter, granulated sugar, and brown sugar until fluffy, about 3 minutes. Add in egg, egg yolk, and vanilla and stir until combined.

2. In a separate large bowl, whisk together flour, cornstarch, baking powder, and salt until well combined.

3. Pour the wet ingredients into the dry ingredients and fold until just combined. Fold in pecans.

4. Cover bowl with plastic wrap, then chill in refrigerator at least 1 hour.

5. Preheat air fryer to 350°F. Cut a piece of parchment to fit air fryer basket.

6. Scoop about 2 tablespoons dough, place on parchment, then gently flatten into a disc about ½" thick. Repeat with remaining dough, leaving 2" of space in between.

7. Place parchment into air fryer basket, working in batches as needed. Bake 8 minutes or until edges are golden brown and the center no longer looks wet. Transfer to a wire rack to cool. Serve warm.

PER SERVING

CALORIES: 233 | FAT: 14g | SODIUM: 207mg | CARBOHYDRATES: 23g | FIBER: 1g | SUGAR: 14g | PROTEIN: 3g

Thumbprint Cookies

These delicate shortbread-like cookies provide a tasty snack. A jam-filled center makes each bite full of delicious fruity flavor. Try swapping out the jam for your favorite kind. Raspberry, blackberry, and apricot are all good options.

Hands-on time: 15 minutes
Cook time: 8 minutes

Yields 8, 1 per serving

- $1/2$ cup salted butter, softened
- $1/2$ cup light brown sugar, packed
- 1 cup all-purpose flour
- $1/2$ teaspoon baking powder
- $1/2$ teaspoon vanilla extract
- 8 teaspoons strawberry jam

1 Preheat air fryer to 350°F. Cut a piece of parchment to fit air fryer basket.

2 In a large bowl, use an electric hand mixer to beat butter and brown sugar until fluffy, about 2 minutes. Add flour, baking powder, and vanilla and mix until well combined.

3 Scoop about 2 tablespoons dough and roll into a ball. Place on parchment. Repeat with remaining dough.

4 Gently press a teaspoon into the center of each dough ball. Place 1 teaspoon jam in each indentation.

5 Place parchment into air fryer basket, working in batches as needed. Bake 8 minutes or until golden brown. Transfer to a wire rack to cool. Serve warm.

PER SERVING

CALORIES: 230 | FAT: 11g | SODIUM: 127mg | CARBOHYDRATES: 30g | FIBER: 1g | SUGAR: 17g | PROTEIN: 2g

Chocolate Caramel-Stuffed Cookies

These ultra-rich cookies are an excellent indulgent treat. Chocolate and caramel always make a delicious combination. This recipe does require chilling time to help give the cookies a firmer structure for holding the caramel, but don't worry, because you can make the dough up to 12 hours ahead of time so it's ready when you are.

Hands-on time: 10 minutes
Cook time: 30 minutes

Yields 12, 1 per serving

1/2 cup salted butter, melted
1/2 cup granulated sugar
1 teaspoon vanilla extract
1 large egg
1 cup all-purpose flour
1/4 cup unsweetened cocoa powder
1 teaspoon baking powder
6 soft baking caramels, halved
1/2 cup pretzels, broken into pieces

1 In a large bowl, use an electric hand mixer to beat butter, sugar, and vanilla until fluffy, about 2 minutes. Mix in egg.

2 In a medium bowl, whisk together flour, cocoa powder, and baking powder until well combined.

3 Add the wet ingredients to the dry ingredients and stir until a soft dough forms.

4 Cover dough with plastic wrap, then place in refrigerator to chill at least 45 minutes.

5 Preheat air fryer to 325°F. Cut a piece of parchment to fit air fryer basket.

6 Scoop about 2 tablespoons dough and roll into a ball. Make an indent in the center and place 1 caramel half. Press dough together to cover caramel. Repeat with remaining dough and caramels.

7 Place crushed pretzels on a plate. Gently press each top of each dough ball in pretzels to coat, then place on parchment.

8 Place parchment into air fryer basket, working in batches as needed. Bake 10 minutes or until set. Transfer to a wire rack and let cool 15 minutes before serving.

PER SERVING

CALORIES: 173 | FAT: 8g | SODIUM: 158mg | CARBOHYDRATES: 23g | FIBER: 1g | SUGAR: 11g | PROTEIN: 2g

White Chocolate Cranberry Biscotti

Biscotti are flat, long cookies that tend to be drier than regular cookies. This makes them perfect for dipping in coffee or hot chocolate. These festive treats are a delicious addition to a holiday gathering plate.

Hands-on time: 10 minutes
Cook time: 20 minutes

Yields 16, 1 per serving

- 1/2 cup salted butter, melted
- 3/4 cup granulated sugar
- 3 cups all-purpose flour
- 2 teaspoons baking powder
- 1 1/2 teaspoons almond extract
- 1/4 cup sweetened dried cranberries
- 1/4 cup white chocolate chips

CUSTOMIZE IT

If you're not a huge fan of cranberries and white chocolate, you can still enjoy this recipe by swapping these out for your favorite flavors. Chocolate chips, slivered almonds, and crushed pistachios are all great substitutes!

1 Preheat air fryer to 320°F. Cut a piece of parchment to fit air fryer basket.

2 In a large bowl, mix butter and sugar. Add flour, baking powder, and almond extract and combine until a soft dough forms.

3 Fold in cranberries and chocolate chips.

4 Separate dough into two evenly sized balls. Press each dough ball into a 5" × 8" rectangle, about 1/2" thick. Place on parchment, leaving 2" of space between the rectangles.

5 Place parchment into air fryer basket, working in batches as needed. Bake 18 minutes or until the center is firm and top is golden brown. Let cool completely, about 2 hours.

6 Preheat air fryer to 400°F. Slice biscotti into 1" pieces diagonally.

7 Place biscotti (cut side up) into air fryer, working in batches as needed.

8 Bake 1 minute per side or until golden brown and crispy. Let cool 10 minutes before serving.

PER SERVING

CALORIES: 193 | FAT: 6g | SODIUM: 109mg | CARBOHYDRATES: 31g | FIBER: 1g | SUGAR: 12g | PROTEIN: 3g

Chocolate Mint Chip Cookies

These soft-baked cookies have golden brown edges and are loaded with delicious peppermint and chocolate flavor in every bite. They're sure to be a hit for your holiday celebrations.

Hands-on time: 10 minutes
Cook time: 30 minutes

Yields 12, 1 per serving

1/2 cup salted butter, softened
1 cup granulated sugar
1 large egg
1 teaspoon vanilla extract
1 cup all-purpose flour
1/3 cup unsweetened cocoa powder
1/2 teaspoon baking soda
1/4 teaspoon salt
1/2 cup mint chips

1 Preheat air fryer to 350°F.

2 In a large bowl, use an electric hand mixer to beat butter and sugar until fluffy, about 2 minutes. Add egg and vanilla, then mix to combine.

3 In a separate large bowl, whisk together flour, cocoa powder, baking soda, and salt.

4 Pour the wet ingredients into the dry ingredients and stir to combine. Fold in mint chips until well combined.

5 Scoop about 2 tablespoons dough, roll into a ball, then gently flatten into a disc about 1/2" thick disc. Repeat with remaining dough.

6 Place cookies into air fryer basket, working in batches as needed. Bake 10 minutes or until edges are set. Transfer to a wire rack to cool. Serve warm.

PER SERVING

CALORIES: 231 | FAT: 11g | SODIUM: 140mg | CARBOHYDRATES: 31g | FIBER: 2g | SUGAR: 22g | PROTEIN: 3g

Double Chocolate Biscotti

If you're a fan of bold flavors, you'll love dunking one of these cookies into your coffee for a delicious mocha bite. These chocolate biscotti are the perfect bite when you want something sweet. Even though they're double chocolate, you'll find they aren't overly sugary, which makes them great for any time of the day.

Hands-on time: 10 minutes
Cook time: 20 minutes

Yields 16, 1 per serving

$1/2$ cup salted butter, melted
1 cup granulated sugar
$1/4$ cup unsweetened dark cocoa powder
3 cups all-purpose flour
2 teaspoons baking powder
1 teaspoon vanilla extract
$1/2$ cup milk chocolate chips

1 Preheat air fryer to 320°F. Cut a piece of parchment to fit air fryer basket.

2 In a large bowl, mix butter and sugar. Add cocoa powder, flour, baking powder, and vanilla and combine until a soft dough forms.

3 Fold in chocolate chips.

4 Separate dough into two evenly sized balls. Press each dough ball into a 5" × 8" rectangle, about $1/2$" thick. Place onto parchment.

5 Place parchment into air fryer basket, working in batches as needed. Bake 18 minutes or until the center is firm. Let cool completely, about 2 hours.

6 Preheat air fryer to 400°F. Slice biscotti into 1" pieces diagonally.

7 Place biscotti (cut side up) into air fryer basket, working in batches as needed.

8 Bake 1 minute per side or until browned and crispy. Let cool 10 minutes before serving.

PER SERVING

CALORIES: 216 | **FAT:** 7g | **SODIUM:** 111mg | **CARBOHYDRATES:** 34g | **FIBER:** 1g | **SUGAR:** 15g | **PROTEIN:** 3g

Oatmeal Chocolate Chip Cookies

These sweet and buttery cookies are the perfect blend of chewy goodness and chocolaty taste. They're golden brown with just a little crunch on the outside. You can use this recipe as a base for adding other tasty mix-ins, from dried cranberries to walnuts.

Hands-on time: 10 minutes
Cook time: 30 minutes

Yields 12, 1 per serving

6 tablespoons salted butter, melted
1/4 cup light brown sugar, packed
2 tablespoons granulated sugar
1 large egg
1 teaspoon vanilla extract
1/2 cup all-purpose flour
1/4 teaspoon salt
1/4 teaspoon baking soda
1 cup quick oats
1/2 cup semisweet chocolate chips

1 Preheat air fryer to 300°F.

2 In a large bowl, use an electric hand mixer to beat butter, brown sugar, granulated sugar, egg, and vanilla until fluffy, about 2 minutes.

3 In a separate large bowl, whisk together flour, salt, baking soda, and oats.

4 Slowly add the wet ingredients to the dry ingredients and stir until combined. Fold in chocolate chips.

5 Scoop about 2 tablespoons dough, roll into a ball, then gently flatten into a disc about 1/2" thick. Repeat with remaining dough.

6 Place cookies into air fryer basket, working in batches as needed. Bake 10 minutes or until lightly browned. Let cool 10 minutes before serving.

PER SERVING

CALORIES: 163 | **FAT:** 8g | **SODIUM:** 128mg | **CARBOHYDRATES:** 20g | **FIBER:** 1g | **SUGAR:** 11g | **PROTEIN:** 2g

Banana Oatmeal Breakfast Cookies

This delicious recipe is low in sugar and is gluten-free. It's a breakfast you can feel good about serving. The only sweeteners in this recipe are honey and bananas, but you'll be surprised at how well those natural sweeteners work here. Since this recipe is only oats, they're a little more textured than a traditional oatmeal cookie, and they come out puffy and cake-like.

Hands-on time: 10 minutes
Cook time: 21 minutes

Yields 12, 1 per serving

2 large ripe bananas, peeled
1 1/2 cups quick oats
1/2 teaspoon ground cinnamon
1 teaspoon vanilla extract
1 tablespoon honey
1/3 cup semisweet chocolate chips

1 Preheat air fryer to 320°F. Cut a piece of parchment to fit air fryer basket.

2 In a medium bowl, mash bananas until mostly smooth. Mix in oats, cinnamon, vanilla, and honey until well combined. Fold in chocolate chips.

3 Scoop about 2 tablespoons dough, roll into a ball, then place on parchment. Gently flatten into a disc about 1/2" thick. Repeat with remaining dough.

4 Place parchment into air fryer basket, working in batches as needed. Bake 7 minutes or until golden brown. Transfer to a wire rack and let cool for 5 minutes. Serve warm.

PER SERVING

CALORIES: 86 | **FAT:** 2g | **SODIUM:** 1mg | **CARBOHYDRATES:** 16g | **FIBER:** 2g | **SUGAR:** 7g | **PROTEIN:** 2g

White Chocolate Cranberry Cookies

There's no denying that cranberry and white chocolate is a power combo. The mild sweetness of the white chocolate tones down the tartness of the cranberries in a way that makes both flavors shine. These soft-baked cookies are great to make in the holiday season when fresh cranberries are easy to find.

Hands-on time: 40 minutes
Cook time: 20 minutes

Yields 12, 1 per serving

- ½ cup salted butter, softened
- ½ cup light brown sugar, packed
- ½ cup granulated sugar
- 1 large egg
- 1 teaspoon vanilla extract
- 1¼ cups all-purpose flour
- ½ teaspoon salt
- ½ teaspoon baking soda
- 1 cup white chocolate chips
- ½ cup sweetened dried cranberries

1 In a large bowl, use an electric hand mixer to beat butter, brown sugar, and granulated sugar until fluffy, about 2 minutes. Add egg and vanilla and mix until fully combined.

2 In a medium bowl, whisk together flour, salt, and baking soda.

3 Add the wet ingredients to the dry ingredients and stir until a soft dough forms. Fold in chocolate chips and cranberries. Cover with plastic wrap and chill in refrigerator 30 minutes.

4 Preheat air fryer to 320°F. Cut a piece of parchment to fit air fryer basket.

5 Scoop 2 tablespoons dough, roll into a ball, then gently flatten into a disc about ½" thick. Place on parchment. Repeat with remaining dough, leaving 2" of space in between.

6 Place parchment into air fryer basket, working in batches as needed. Bake 10 minutes or until edges are browned. Let cool 10 minutes before serving.

PER SERVING

CALORIES: 280 | FAT: 12g | SODIUM: 231mg | CARBOHYDRATES: 40g | FIBER: 1g | SUGAR: 29g | PROTEIN: 3g

Oatmeal Maple Pecan Cookies

Maple is a delicious flavor you might not think to add into cookies often. These cookies taste like a delicious bite of morning oatmeal. They're soft and chewy with just a hint of crunch from the golden edges and pecans.

Hands-on time: 10 minutes
Cook time: 30 minutes

Yields 12 cookies, 1 per serving

---

6 tablespoons salted butter, melted
1/4 cup light brown sugar, packed
2 tablespoons pure maple syrup
1 large egg
1 teaspoon vanilla extract
1/2 teaspoon maple extract
1/2 cup all-purpose flour
1/4 teaspoon salt
1/4 teaspoon baking soda
1 cup quick oats
1/2 cup chopped pecans

1 Preheat air fryer to 300°F.

2 In a medium bowl, mix butter, brown sugar, maple syrup, egg, vanilla, and maple extract until well combined.

3 In a separate medium bowl, whisk together flour, salt, baking soda, and oats.

4 Slowly add the wet ingredients to the dry ingredients and stir until combined. Fold in pecans.

5 Scoop about 2 tablespoons dough, roll into a ball, then gently flatten into a disc about 1/2" thick. Repeat with remaining dough.

6 Place cookies into air fryer basket, working in batches as needed. Bake 10 minutes or until lightly browned. Let cool 10 minutes before serving.

PER SERVING

CALORIES: 160 | **FAT:** 9g | **SODIUM:** 7mg | **CARBOHYDRATES:** 16g | **FIBER:** 1g | **SUGAR:** 7g | **PROTEIN:** 2g

Pumpkin White Chocolate Chip Cookies

Pumpkin is one of the most popular flavors of fall, and if you're a fan, this recipe is a must. These soft cookies are filled with spices that bring out all the best fall flavors. The brown sugar gives these cookies the extra depth they need to complement the spices and take these to the next level.

Hands-on time: 15 minutes
Cook time: 24 minutes

Yields 12, 1 per serving

1¼ cups all-purpose flour
½ teaspoon baking soda
¼ teaspoon baking powder
1 tablespoon pumpkin pie spice
½ tablespoon ground cinnamon
½ teaspoon salt
¼ cup salted butter, softened
½ cup light brown sugar, packed
¼ cup granulated sugar
1 large egg
1 teaspoon vanilla extract
1 cup white chocolate chips

CHOCOLATE CHIP SWAP

If you don't like white chocolate chips, that doesn't mean you need to miss out on this recipe. Swap the white chocolate with milk chocolate and see how you like it. It's a much richer flavor combined with pumpkin, but you may find it's surprisingly delicious.

1 In a medium bowl, whisk together flour, baking soda, baking powder, pumpkin pie spice, cinnamon, and salt until well combined.

2 In a separate medium bowl, mix butter, brown sugar, granulated sugar, egg, and vanilla until well combined.

3 Add the wet ingredients to the dry ingredients, stirring well until a soft dough forms. Fold in white chocolate chips. Cover with plastic wrap and chill in refrigerator at least 1 hour.

4 Preheat air fryer to 350°F. Cut a piece of parchment to fit air fryer basket and spray lightly with cooking spray.

5 Scoop about 2 tablespoons dough, roll into a ball, then gently flatten into a disc about ½" thick. Place on parchment. Repeat with remaining dough, leaving at least 2" of space between cookies.

6 Place parchment into air fryer basket, working in batches as needed. Bake 12 minutes or until edges are golden brown and the center no longer appears wet. Let cool 10 minutes before serving.

PER SERVING

CALORIES: 199 | FAT: 8g | SODIUM: 210mg | CARBOHYDRATES: 28g | FIBER: 1g | SUGAR: 17g | PROTEIN: 3g

Peppermint White Chocolate Chip Cookies

Make a batch of these to enjoy during your winter holiday movie marathons! In less than 30 minutes, you'll be enjoying these gooey white chocolate chip cookies that have just the right amount of peppermint crunch. If you're feeling festive, you can also use crushed-up candy canes in red and green for a hint of color.

Hands-on time: 15 minutes
Cook time: 8 minutes

Yields 12, 1 per serving

- ½ cup salted butter, softened
- ½ cup light brown sugar, packed
- ¼ cup granulated sugar
- 1 large egg
- 1 teaspoon vanilla extract
- 1 cup all-purpose flour
- 1 tablespoon cornstarch
- ¼ teaspoon baking soda
- ½ teaspoon salt
- ½ cup white chocolate chips
- ½ cup crushed peppermint candies

1 Preheat air fryer to 350°F. Cut a piece of parchment to fit air fryer basket and spray it lightly with cooking spray.

2 In a large bowl, use an electric hand mixer to beat butter, brown sugar, and granulated sugar until light and fluffy, about 2 minutes. Mix in egg and vanilla until well combined.

3 In a separate large bowl, whisk together flour, cornstarch, baking soda, and salt until well combined.

4 Add the wet ingredients to the dry ingredients and use a rubber spatula to stir until just combined. Fold in white chocolate chips and peppermint candies.

5 Scoop about 2 tablespoons dough, roll into a ball, then place on parchment, leaving at least 2" of space between each cookie. Repeat with remaining dough.

6 Place parchment into air fryer basket, working in batches as needed. Bake 8 minutes or until edges are golden brown. Let cookies cool 15 minutes. Serve warm.

PER SERVING

CALORIES: 236 | FAT: 10g | SODIUM: 198mg | CARBOHYDRATES: 33g | FIBER: 0g | SUGAR: 23g | PROTEIN: 2g

Confetti Cake Mix Cookies

This is great to make with the family. They're an easy recipe that the kids will be excited to help make, without the hassle of multiple measured-out ingredients. If you're a fan of cake pops, you'll love the texture of these super-moist cookies.

Hands-on time: 10 minutes
Cook time: 10 minutes

Yields 12, 1 per serving

1 (18.25-ounce) box vanilla
    cake mix
2 large eggs
$1/2$ cup vegetable oil
$1/2$ cup rainbow sprinkles,
    divided

1 Preheat air fryer to 350°F. Cut two pieces of parchment to fit air fryer basket.

2 In a large bowl, mix cake mix, eggs, and oil together. Fold in $1/4$ cup sprinkles.

3 Scoop about 2 tablespoons dough, roll into a ball, then gently flatten into a disc about $1/2$" thick. Repeat with remaining dough, leaving 2" of space in between.

4 Place remaining $1/4$ cup sprinkles on a plate and press one side of each cookie into sprinkles to coat. Place on parchment (with sprinkle side up). Repeat with remaining dough.

5 Place parchment into air fryer basket, working in batches as needed. Bake 10 minutes or until golden at edges. Transfer to a wire rack to cool. Serve warm.

PER SERVING

CALORIES: 306 | FAT: 15g | SODIUM: 298mg | CARBOHYDRATES: 43g | FIBER: 0g | SUGAR: 29g | PROTEIN: 3g

Double Chocolate Cake Mix Cookies

This cookie is so moist, you could almost consider it a truffle. The chocolate pudding is the secret ingredient that boosts flavor, but it also makes the most deliciously moist recipe you could imagine from a cake mix. Each soft bite is filled with rich flavor.

Hands-on time: 10 minutes
Cook time: 15 minutes

Yields 12, 1 per serving

1 (15.25-ounce) box chocolate cake mix
1 (3-ounce) box instant chocolate pudding
½ cup salted butter, melted
2 large eggs
1 cup semisweet chocolate chips

1 Preheat air fryer to 350°F. Cut two pieces of parchment to fit air fryer basket.

2 In a large bowl, whisk together cake mix, pudding mix, butter, and eggs until well combined. Fold in chocolate chips.

3 Scoop about 2 tablespoons dough, roll into a ball, then gently flatten into a disc about ½" thick. Place on parchment. Repeat with remaining dough, leaving 2" of space in between.

4 Place parchment into air fryer basket, working in batches as needed. Bake 15 minutes or until edges are set. Transfer to a wire rack and let cool 10 minutes before serving.

PER SERVING

CALORIES: 320 | FAT: 15g | SODIUM: 476mg | CARBOHYDRATES: 45g | FIBER: 2g | SUGAR: 27g | PROTEIN: 4g

Coconut Macaroons

These golden brown cookies are perfect for coconut lovers. In just 15 minutes, these caramelized cookies are ready to eat. They are soft and thick in the center, while the outside remains slightly crispy. These require just a few ingredients, so they're perfect in a pinch.

Hands-on time: 10 minutes
Cook time: 18 minutes

Yields 12, 1 per serving

- 3 cups sweetened shredded coconut
- 2 large egg whites
- $1/3$ cup light brown sugar, packed
- 1 teaspoon vanilla extract
- $1/4$ teaspoon salt

1 Preheat air fryer to 350°F. Cut two pieces of parchment to fit air fryer basket.

2 Place coconut in a 6" round baking pan and bake 3 minutes, stirring every minute until coconut is lightly toasted. Reduce air fryer temperature to 300°F.

3 In a large bowl, use an electric hand mixer on high speed to whip egg whites until stiff peaks form, about 3 minutes. Add brown sugar, vanilla, and salt and continue whipping until thick, about 3 minutes. Fold toasted coconut into egg white mixture.

4 Place heaping spoonfuls of mixture on parchment, leaving at least 1" of space between cookies.

5 Place parchment into air fryer basket, working in batches as needed. Bake 5 minutes or until firm and lightly golden. Transfer to a wire rack and let cool 5 minutes before serving.

PER SERVING

CALORIES: 123 | FAT: 6g | SODIUM: 119mg | CARBOHYDRATES: 17g | FIBER: 2g | SUGAR: 14g | PROTEIN: 1g

5

Bars and Brownies

There's more than one way to make a brownie. In fact, the possibilities are so endless that this jam-packed chapter just scratches the surface. Bars and brownies are the perfect treat to share. Whether you're making dessert for your family or brainstorming a dish to bring to the potluck at work, this chapter has you covered.

One important note about this chapter is that most of the recipes were created in an 8" × 8" pan. However, air fryers vary greatly in size, so that may not fit the size of your air fryer. Consider a 6" cake pan as a substitute for the larger square pan in those cases. This means you may need to work in batches. Nonetheless, the recipes in this chapter are simple and delicious no matter what size pan you cook them in.

This chapter is full of perfect handheld recipes such as Raspberry Lemon Bars and Chocolate Hazelnut Brownie Bites to satisfy your sweet tooth any time of day.

Raspberry Lemon Bars

This recipe is a flavorful twist on lemon bars. Each smooth bite is bursting with sweetness and a hint of tartness. The crust is made with premade dough as a time-saver, but feel free to use a shortbread crust if you prefer.

Hands-on time: 15 minutes
Cook time: 30 minutes

Serves 9

1 (8-ounce) tube premade sugar cookie dough
3 large eggs
3/4 cup granulated sugar
2 tablespoons all-purpose flour
1 cup raspberries
1/4 cup lemon juice
2 tablespoons lemon zest
2 tablespoons confectioners' sugar

1 Preheat air fryer to 350°F. Spray an 8" × 8" baking pan with cooking spray and line with parchment.

2 Press dough into pan and bake 5 minutes or until lightly browned. Let cool 10 minutes. Reduce air fryer temperature to 300°F.

3 In a medium bowl, whisk together eggs, granulated sugar, flour, raspberries, lemon juice, and lemon zest until well combined. Pour mixture into cooled crust.

4 Place pan into air fryer basket. Bake 25 minutes or until edges and center are set. Let cool 30 minutes, then sprinkle with confectioners' sugar and refrigerate at least 4 hours until fully chilled before slicing into bars and serving.

PER SERVING

CALORIES: 155 | FAT: 6g | SODIUM: 97mg | CARBOHYDRATES: 21g | FIBER: 1g | SUGAR: 12g | PROTEIN: 3g

Peanut Butter and Jelly Bars

Your favorite childhood sandwich, now in bar form. This dessert will bring back all the nostalgia. This recipe uses an oat bar base topped with creamy peanut butter and jelly.

Hands-on time: 10 minutes
Cook time: 15 minutes

Serves 12

½ cup salted butter, softened
½ cup peanut butter
½ cup light brown sugar, packed
½ cup quick oats
1 teaspoon baking powder
½ teaspoon baking soda
½ teaspoon salt
½ cup grape jelly

1 Preheat air fryer to 350°F. Spray an 8" × 8" baking dish with cooking spray.

2 In a medium bowl, mix butter, peanut butter, and brown sugar until smooth and well combined.

3 Stir in oats, baking powder, baking soda, and salt until a soft batter forms. Pour batter into prepared pan.

4 Place small spoonfuls of jelly in nine separate spots across top, then use a knife to swirl jelly into the batter.

5 Place pan into air fryer basket. Bake 15 minutes or until sides are golden brown. Let cool 15 minutes. Slice into bars and serve warm.

PER SERVING

CALORIES: 216 | FAT: 12g | SODIUM: 303mg | CARBOHYDRATES: 23g | FIBER: 1g | SUGAR: 17g | PROTEIN: 3g

Brownies

There's nothing like a warm brownie and a scoop of ice cream. These brownies come together in no time, which makes them perfect for dessert while dinner is cooking in the oven. They're fudgy and loaded with gooey chocolate goodness.

Hands-on time: 10 minutes
Cook time: 25 minutes

Serves 9

1 cup all-purpose flour
1/2 cup unsweetened cocoa powder
2 teaspoons baking powder
1/2 cup unsalted butter, softened
1 cup granulated sugar
1 teaspoon vanilla extract
2 large eggs, whisked
1 cup semisweet chocolate chips

1. Preheat air fryer to 300°F. Line an 8" × 8" baking dish with parchment and spray with cooking spray.

2. In a large bowl, whisk together flour, cocoa powder, and baking powder.

3. In a separate large bowl, use an electric handheld mixer to cream butter, sugar, and vanilla until fluffy, about 3 minutes.

4. Add the wet ingredients to the dry ingredients and mix until just combined. Pour in eggs and stir to combine. Fold in chocolate chips.

5. Pour batter in prepared pan.

6. Place pan into air fryer basket. Bake 25 minutes or until a toothpick inserted into the center comes out clean. Let cool 10 minutes before serving.

PER SERVING

CALORIES: 352 | **FAT:** 17g | **SODIUM:** 129mg | **CARBOHYDRATES:** 49g | **FIBER:** 3g | **SUGAR:** 33g | **PROTEIN:** 5g

Coconut-Stuffed Brownies

If you're a fan of coconut and chocolate candy bars, you'll love this recipe! This stuffed brownie is packed with creamy coconut. Each bite is filled with moist, chewy brownie and a yummy coconut center.

Hands-on time: 15 minutes
Cook time: 25 minutes

Serves 9

- ½ cup all-purpose flour
- ½ cup unsweetened cocoa powder
- 1 tablespoon baking powder
- ½ cup granulated sugar
- 1 teaspoon vanilla extract
- ¼ cup vegetable oil
- 1 large egg
- 1 cup sweetened shredded coconut
- ½ cup sweetened condensed milk

1 Preheat air fryer to 320°F. Spray an 8" × 8" baking dish with cooking spray.

2 In a medium bowl, whisk together flour, cocoa powder, baking powder, and sugar until well combined.

3 Whisk in vanilla, oil, and egg until a smooth batter forms.

4 In a separate medium bowl, mix coconut and sweetened condensed milk.

5 Pour half of the chocolate batter in prepared baking pan. Place spoonfuls of coconut mixture on top, gently spreading into an even layer. Pour remaining chocolate on top.

6 Place dish into air fryer basket. Bake 25 minutes or until edges are firm and a toothpick inserted into the center comes out clean. Let cool 30 minutes before serving.

PER SERVING

CALORIES: 296 | **FAT:** 13g | **SODIUM:** 241mg | **CARBOHYDRATES:** 43g | **FIBER:** 3g | **SUGAR:** 33g | **PROTEIN:** 5g

Hot Fudge Brownies

This recipe upgrades the classic boxed brownie mix into a delectable dessert perfect for chocolate lovers. It's great for cozy nights at home but can be dressed up for any occasion. Add your favorite sundae toppings such as chopped nuts or sprinkles for an extra crunch.

Hands-on time: 10 minutes
Cook time: 20 minutes

Yields 6, 1 per serving

1½ cups boxed brownie mix
2 large eggs
½ cup sweetened condensed milk
¼ cup vegetable oil
¼ cup brewed coffee, cooled
½ cup hot fudge topping, warmed
8 tablespoons whipped cream

EXTRA BROWNIE MIX
You'll realize when making this recipe that you end up with extra boxed mix. You can store this leftover dry brownie mix in a sealed bag and use it the next time you make this recipe. Alternatively, you can double this recipe to use the entire box. It never hurts to have extra brownies!

1 Preheat air fryer to 320°F. Spray six 4" ramekins with cooking spray.

2 In a medium bowl, whisk together brownie mix, eggs, sweetened condensed milk, oil, and coffee until smooth.

3 Pour ⅓ cup batter in each prepared ramekin.

4 Place ramekins into air fryer basket, working in batches as needed. Bake 10 minutes or until edges are firm and a toothpick inserted into the center comes out clean. Let cool 10 minutes and slice into bars.

5 Pour 1 heaping tablespoon warmed hot fudge on each brownie. Top with whipped cream immediately before serving. Serve warm.

PER SERVING

CALORIES: 450 | FAT: 20g | SODIUM: 258mg | CARBOHYDRATES: 60g | FIBER: 1g | SUGAR: 23g | PROTEIN: 7g

Easy Red Velvet Cheesecake Swirl Bars

When you're short on time, box mixes are a real time-saver. These ultra-moist bars have a delicious swirl of cheesecake, making them feel like a huge upgrade from a simple boxed mix cake. Using vegetable oil creates a fudgy brownie texture that you'll love.

Hands-on time: 10 minutes
Cook time: 20 minutes

Serves 9

1 (15.25-ounce) box red
    velvet cake mix
1/3 cup vegetable oil
2 large eggs
1 teaspoon vanilla extract
4 ounces cream cheese,
    softened
1/4 cup granulated sugar
2 tablespoons whole milk

1 Preheat air fryer to 300°F. Spray an 8" × 8" baking pan with cooking spray.

2 In a large bowl, stir cake mix, oil, eggs, and vanilla until well combined. Pour batter in prepared pan.

3 In a medium bowl, mix cream cheese, sugar, and milk until smooth.

4 Place cream cheese mixture on top in twelve spoonfuls, then use a knife to swirl cheesecake mixture into cake batter.

5 Place dish into air fryer basket. Bake 20 minutes or until edges are browned and a toothpick inserted into the center comes out clean. Let cool 10 minutes before slicing and serving.

PER SERVING

CALORIES: 358 | FAT: 18g | SODIUM: 431mg | CARBOHYDRATES: 43g | FIBER: 1g | SUGAR: 26g | PROTEIN: 4g

Chocolate Hazelnut Brownie Bites

These are the perfect pick-me-up bites. Each is filled with delicious hazelnut spread. The outside is chewy, but the center stays moist. Top them with a little whipped cream or enjoy them with a mini scoop of ice cream for an extra-special treat.

Hands-on time: 10 minutes
Cook time: 10 minutes

Yields 12, 1 per serving

1 cup chocolate hazelnut spread
2 tablespoons unsweetened cocoa powder
$1/2$ cup granulated sugar
1 large egg
$1/2$ cup all-purpose flour
$1/2$ cup hazelnuts, chopped

HAZELNUT SPREAD

Hazelnut spread often goes by its brand name, Nutella. But that's not the only kind available. There are lots of great store-brand options that will work perfectly in this recipe.

1   Preheat air fryer to 300°F. Spray twelve foil baking liners with cooking spray.

2   In a large bowl, combine hazelnut spread, cocoa powder, sugar, and egg.

3   Mix in flour until just combined, then fold in hazelnuts.

4   Scoop 3 tablespoons mixture in each liner.

5   Place liners into air fryer basket, working in batches as needed. Bake 10 minutes or until edges are firm and the center of each is set and a toothpick comes out clean. Let cool 20 minutes before slicing and serving.

PER SERVING

CALORIES: 222 | **FAT:** 10g | **SODIUM:** 16mg | **CARBOHYDRATES:** 29g | **FIBER:** 2g | **SUGAR:** 22g | **PROTEIN:** 3g

White Chocolate Macadamia Nut Blondies

While brownies are a classic, sometimes you want a bit of variety. That's where blondies, with their rich and buttery taste, come in. They're soft and chewy like a brownie but with a lightened-up flavor and a bit of crunch from the macadamia nuts.

Hands-on time: 15 minutes
Cook time: 35 minutes

Serves 9

1 cup granulated sugar
1/2 cup salted butter, softened
1 tablespoon vanilla extract
2 large eggs
1 1/2 cups all-purpose flour
1 1/2 teaspoons baking powder
1 teaspoon salt
1/2 cup white chocolate chips
1/2 cup macadamia nuts, chopped

1 Preheat air fryer to 300°F. Line an 8" × 8" baking pan with parchment and spray with cooking spray.

2 In a large bowl, use an electric hand mixer to cream together sugar, butter, and vanilla until fluffy, about 2 minutes. Add eggs and mix until combined.

3 In a small bowl, whisk together flour, baking powder, and salt.

4 Slowly incorporate the dry ingredients into the wet ingredients, gently stirring until well combined. Fold in white chocolate chips and macadamia nuts. Pour batter in prepared pan.

5 Place pan into air fryer basket. Bake 35 minutes or until edges are golden brown and a toothpick inserted into the center comes out clean. Let cool 10 minutes before slicing and serving.

PER SERVING

CALORIES: 375 | FAT: 19g | SODIUM: 445mg | CARBOHYDRATES: 45g | FIBER: 1g | SUGAR: 28g | PROTEIN: 5g

Raspberry Swirl Cheesecake Bars

This recipe is yummy for weeknights and special occasions alike! These bars have a pop of flavor that takes them to the next level. The crumbly crust and rich, creamy filling come together quickly, but these bars do need chilling time, so be sure to plan ahead.

Hands-on time: 15 minutes
Cook time: 23 minutes

Serves 9

12 graham cracker sheets
3 tablespoons salted butter, melted
16 ounces cream cheese, softened
$1/2$ cup granulated sugar
$1/4$ cup sour cream
2 teaspoons vanilla extract
$1/2$ teaspoon lemon juice
2 large eggs, whisked
$1/4$ cup raspberry preserves

1 Preheat air fryer to 300°F. Line an 8" × 8" baking dish with parchment and spray with cooking spray.

2 Place graham crackers into a food processor and pulse ten times or until mostly broken down. Add butter and pulse five times or until a sand-like texture that sticks together when pressed between your fingers forms.

3 Firmly press crust mixture into bottom of prepared dish. Place pan into air fryer basket. Bake 5 minutes and let cool for 5 minutes.

4 In a large bowl, mix cream cheese and sugar until completely smooth. Stir in sour cream, then add vanilla and lemon juice and stir until well combined. Add eggs and stir until just combined.

5 Pour mixture in baked crust. Place spoonfuls of raspberry preserves around the top, then use a knife to gently swirl into cheesecake batter.

6 Place cheesecake into air fryer basket. Bake 18 minutes or until edges are set and the middle jiggles only slightly when moved. Let cool 15 minutes inside air fryer then move to counter to cool 2 hours, then refrigerate at least 6 hours before slicing and serving.

PER SERVING

CALORIES: 373 | FAT: 22g | SODIUM: 310mg | CARBOHYDRATES: 34g | FIBER: 1g | SUGAR: 22g | PROTEIN: 5g

Key Lime Pie Bars

Citrus is always fun and refreshing, and so are these bars. The crumbly crust and rich, creamy filling go perfectly together. The lime is just the right amount of tangy to make this summertime dessert the star of the show.

Hands-on time: 15 minutes
Cook time: 20 minutes

Serves 9

8 graham cracker sheets
3 tablespoons salted butter, melted
3 large egg yolks, whisked
1 (14-ounce) can sweetened condensed milk
½ cup granulated sugar
1¾ cups lime juice
1 tablespoon fresh lime zest

SEASONAL LIMES

In the off-season, it can be hard to find juicy limes, depending on where you live. You can use bottled lime juice for this recipe, but it's important to keep in mind the flavor may taste a little more artificial.

1 Preheat air fryer to 320°F. Line an 8" × 8" baking pan with parchment and lightly spray with cooking spray.

2 Place graham crackers into a food processor and pulse ten times or until mostly broken down. Add butter and pulse five times or until a sand-like texture that sticks together when pressed between your fingers forms.

3 Firmly press crust mixture into the bottom of prepared pan. Place pan into air fryer basket. Bake 5 minutes.

4 In a large bowl, whisk together egg yolks, sweetened condensed milk, sugar, lime juice, and lime zest until well combined and smooth. Pour mixture in baked crust.

5 Place pan into air fryer basket. Bake 15 minutes or until edges have browned and the center is set. Let cool 1 hour, then refrigerate 4 hours or until completely chilled before serving.

PER SERVING

CALORIES: 301 | FAT: 10g | SODIUM: 147mg | CARBOHYDRATES: 49g | FIBER: 1g | SUGAR: 39g | PROTEIN: 5g

Pineapple Coconut Bars

If you're looking for something different that doesn't have any chocolate, these firm bars are for you. They're filled with citrus flavor and pineapple in each bite.

Hands-on time: 10 minutes
Cook time: 30 minutes

Serves 6

¼ cup salted butter, softened

¼ cup light brown sugar, packed

½ cup plus 2 tablespoons all-purpose flour, divided

½ cup canned crushed pineapple, drained

½ cup sweetened shredded coconut

½ cup granulated sugar

1 large egg

1 tablespoon orange zest

2 tablespoons orange juice

1 teaspoon vanilla extract

EXTRA COCONUT FLAVOR

Coconut loses a little flavor when cooked. If you're a coconut superfan, try adding ¼ teaspoon coconut extract to ensure a strong coconut taste.

1   Preheat air fryer to 325°F. Spray a 6" round baking pan with cooking spray.

2   In a large bowl, use an electric hand mixer to beat butter and brown sugar until well combined and fluffy, about 2 minutes. Mix in ½ cup flour until a soft dough forms.

3   Press dough into bottom of prepared pan. Place pan into air fryer basket. Bake 5 minutes, then let cool 5 minutes.

4   In a medium bowl, mix pineapple, shredded coconut, granulated sugar, egg, orange zest, orange juice, and vanilla until well combined. Mix in remaining 2 tablespoons flour. Pour mixture in baked crust.

5   Place pan into air fryer basket. Bake 25 minutes or until top is golden brown and filling jiggles only slightly. Let cool 30 minutes, then refrigerate at least 2 hours until completely chilled. Serve chilled.

PER SERVING

CALORIES: 263 | **FAT:** 10g | **SODIUM:** 95mg | **CARBOHYDRATES:** 41g | **FIBER:** 1g | **SUGAR:** 31g | **PROTEIN:** 3g

Magic Bars

Sometimes you're in the mood for something ultra-sweet. These bars are full of all the best flavors: gooey caramel, decadent chocolate, and a sprinkle of salt from the pecans. Atop a soft, shortbread-style crust. These bars are the perfect treat for weekends and movie nights.

Hands-on time: 10 minutes
Cook time: 20 minutes

Serves 9

1/2 cup salted butter, melted
1/4 cup confectioners' sugar
1 cup all-purpose flour
1/2 cup caramel sauce
1/4 cup chopped pecans
1/2 cup semisweet chocolate chips

A LITTLE EXTRA MAGIC

Part of the magic in these bars is that you can customize them however you like. Try toasting shredded coconut, swapping the pecans for peanuts, or even changing up the chocolate chips for dark, white, or milk chocolate.

1 Preheat air fryer to 320°F. Line an 8" × 8" baking pan with parchment.

2 In a medium bowl, mix butter, confectioners' sugar, and flour. Press crust mixture into prepared pan. Place pan into air fryer basket. Bake 10 minutes or until lightly golden brown.

3 Pour caramel over crust and spread evenly. Sprinkle pecans and chocolate chips over caramel.

4 Place pan into air fryer basket. Bake 10 minutes or until chocolate is melted. Let cool 10 minutes before slicing and serving.

PER SERVING

CALORIES: 266 | FAT: 15g | SODIUM: 145mg | CARBOHYDRATES: 32g | FIBER: 1g | SUGAR: 8g | PROTEIN: 3g

Brown Sugar Blondies

These blondies are amazing all on their own, but you can include your favorite add-ins such as crushed candy, chocolate chips, or chopped walnuts.

Hands-on time: 15 minutes
Cook time: 35 minutes

Serves 12

1/2 cup salted butter, softened
1 1/2 cups light brown sugar, packed
2 large eggs
1 tablespoon vanilla extract
1 1/2 cups all-purpose flour
1 1/2 teaspoons baking powder
1 teaspoon salt

1 Preheat air fryer to 300°F. Line an 8" × 8" pan with parchment.

2 In a large bowl, use an electric hand mixer to cream together butter and brown sugar.

3 Stir in eggs and vanilla until combined. Add flour, baking powder, and salt and stir until well combined. Add mixture to prepared pan.

4 Place pan into air fryer basket. Bake 35 minutes or until edges are golden brown and a toothpick inserted into the center comes out clean. Let cool completely before slicing and serving.

PER SERVING

CALORIES: 244 | FAT: 8g | SODIUM: 335mg | CARBOHYDRATES: 39g | FIBER: 0g | SUGAR: 27g | PROTEIN: 3g

Peanut Butter Blondies

These blondies are dense, chewy, and full of peanut butter flavor, and they're simple to make.

Hands-on time: 15 minutes
Cook time: 45 minutes

Serves 9

1/2 cup salted butter, softened
1 1/2 cups light brown sugar, packed
1 tablespoon vanilla extract
1 large egg
1/2 cup peanut butter
1 teaspoon salt
3/4 cup all-purpose flour

1 Preheat air fryer to 300°F. Spray an 8" × 8" baking dish with cooking spray.

2 In a large bowl, use an electric hand mixer to beat butter, brown sugar, and vanilla until fluffy, about 2 minutes.

3 Mix in egg and peanut butter until well combined. Add salt and flour and mix until smooth. Place dough in prepared dish.

4 Place dish into air fryer basket. Bake 45 minutes or until golden brown and a toothpick inserted into the center comes out clean. Let cool for 20 minutes before slicing and serving.

PER SERVING

CALORIES: 365 | FAT: 17g | SODIUM: 418mg | CARBOHYDRATES: 47g | FIBER: 1g | SUGAR: 37g | PROTEIN: 5g

Pumpkin Shortbread Bars

This recipe showcases all the flavors of pumpkin pie in an easy-to-make bar! These cook in less time than a pumpkin pie but have all the same flavor. From the buttery crust to the smooth, spiced filling, these delicious bars will be your new fall favorite.

Hands-on time: 15 minutes
Cook time: 24 minutes

Serves 12

- 1/2 cup salted butter, softened
- 3/4 cup granulated sugar, divided
- 2 cups all-purpose flour, divided
- 1 cup pure pumpkin purée
- 2 large eggs
- 2 teaspoons vanilla extract, divided
- 1 cup light brown sugar, packed
- 1/2 teaspoon salt
- 1 tablespoon ground cinnamon
- 1/2 teaspoon ground cloves
- 1/4 cup salted butter, cold

1 Preheat air fryer to 350°F. Spray an 8" × 8" baking dish with cooking spray.

2 In a medium bowl, mix softened butter, 1/2 cup granulated sugar, and 1 cup flour until a soft dough forms. Press dough into the bottom of prepared dish.

3 Place dish into air fryer. Bake 12 minutes or until golden brown, and let cool for 5 minutes.

4 In a medium bowl, mix pumpkin, eggs, 1 teaspoon vanilla, brown sugar, 1/2 cup flour, salt, cinnamon, and cloves until well combined. Pour mixture in baked crust.

5 In a medium bowl, mix remaining 1/2 cup flour, cold butter, remaining 1 teaspoon vanilla, and remaining 1/4 cup granulated sugar until a coarse crumb forms. Sprinkle mixture over pumpkin filling.

6 Place pan into air fryer basket. Bake 12 minutes or until top is golden brown and the center no longer jiggles. Let cool at least 10 minutes before slicing and serving.

PER SERVING

CALORIES: 319 | **FAT:** 12g | **SODIUM:** 206mg | **CARBOHYDRATES:** 49g | **FIBER:** 1g | **SUGAR:** 31g | **PROTEIN:** 4g

Cookies and Cream Bars

Cookies and Cream Bars aren't as common as other bars, like brownies, but they're just as easy and delicious! Stand out at the bake sale with these bars. They are soft and creamy with a perfect bite of cookie crunch.

Hands-on time: 15 minutes
Cook time: 16 minutes

Serves 9

¼ cup salted butter, softened
4 ounces cream cheese, softened
½ tablespoon vanilla extract
1½ cups granulated sugar
1 large egg
1 cup all-purpose flour
½ teaspoon salt
10 chocolate sandwich cookies, crushed

1 Preheat air fryer to 320°F. Line an 8" × 8" baking pan with parchment.

2 In a large bowl, mix butter, cream cheese, vanilla, and sugar until well combined and smooth. Mix in egg, then add flour and salt and mix again.

3 Gently fold in crushed cookies. Place mixture in prepared pan.

4 Place pan into air fryer basket. Bake 16 minutes or until edges are browned and set and a toothpick inserted into the center comes out clean. Let cool at least 30 minutes before serving.

PER SERVING

CALORIES: 339 | **FAT:** 11g | **SODIUM:** 275mg | **CARBOHYDRATES:** 54g | **FIBER:** 1g | **SUGAR:** 39g | **PROTEIN:** 4g

Caramel Apple Crisp Bars

This twist on traditional apple crisp is loaded with even more flavor. The golden brown crunch on top gives every bite yummy texture and flavor. The canned cinnamon roll crust on these is a great way to add some flavor without much extra effort.

Hands-on time: 10 minutes
Cook time: 20 minutes

Serves 9

1 (16.5-ounce) tube cinnamon rolls
2 Granny Smith apples, cored and sliced
1 cup caramel sauce
1 cup old-fashioned oats
½ cup light brown sugar, packed
¼ cup salted butter, melted

APPLE FLAVOR

If you don't enjoy a tart apple such as Granny Smith, try this recipe with a sweeter variety. Fuji and Honeycrisp are sweeter than green apples but have just a hint of tartness to add brightness to the recipe.

1 Preheat air fryer to 320°F. Spray an 8" × 8" baking pan with cooking spray.

2 Press cinnamon roll dough into prepared pan and poke dough with a fork in several places. Place pan into air fryer basket. Bake 10 minutes or until golden brown.

3 Place apples on top of crust and drizzle with caramel.

4 In a medium bowl, mix oats, brown sugar, and butter until mixture is a sand-like consistency, then sprinkle on top of apples and caramel.

5 Place pan into air fryer basket. Bake 10 minutes or until topping is golden brown and apples are softened. Slice and serve warm with icing included with cinnamon rolls.

PER SERVING

CALORIES: 418 | **FAT:** 7g | **SODIUM:** 576mg | **CARBOHYDRATES:** 76g | **FIBER:** 3g | **SUGAR:** 27g | **PROTEIN:** 5g

Raspberry Crumble Bars

This recipe is the perfect summertime treat. The raspberries turn into a delicious sauce that is sandwiched between two chewy oat layers. The pop of flavor from the fruit makes each buttery bite of these bars extra delicious.

Hands-on time: 15 minutes
Cook time: 20 minutes

Serves 9

- ³/₄ cup instant oats
- ³/₄ cup all-purpose flour
- ¹/₂ cup light brown sugar, packed
- ¹/₄ cup salted butter, softened
- 1 teaspoon baking powder
- 1 cup raspberries
- ¹/₄ cup granulated sugar
- 1 tablespoon cornstarch

1 Preheat air fryer to 320°F. Spray an 8" × 8" baking dish with cooking spray.

2 In a large bowl, mix oats, flour, brown sugar, butter, and baking powder. Reserve ¹/₂ cup mixture, then press remaining mixture into prepared dish. Place dish into air fryer basket. Bake 5 minutes or until golden brown.

3 In a medium bowl, toss raspberries, granulated sugar, and cornstarch, then place in baked crust. Scatter reserved crust mixture on top of raspberries.

4 Place dish into air fryer basket. Bake 15 minutes or until golden brown. Let cool 20 minutes before serving.

PER SERVING

CALORIES: 186 | FAT: 5g | SODIUM: 98mg | CARBOHYDRATES: 33g | FIBER: 2g | SUGAR: 18g | PROTEIN: 2g

Maple Pecan Bars

If you love pecan pie, these bars will be a new favorite. They have all the wonderful flavor of the pie you're familiar with but with a buttery shortbread crust. The filling is chewy, sticky, and rich in flavor.

Hands-on time: 10 minutes
Cook time: 25 minutes

Serves 9

1 cup salted butter, softened, divided
1 cup light brown sugar, packed, divided
1 cup all-purpose flour
1/4 cup pure maple syrup
1/4 cup heavy whipping cream
1 teaspoon vanilla extract
1 1/2 cups chopped pecans
1/2 teaspoon salt

1 Preheat air fryer to 320°F. Spray an 8" × 8" baking pan with cooking spray.

2 In a medium bowl, mix 1/2 cup butter, 1/2 cup brown sugar, and flour until a soft dough forms. Press dough into the bottom of prepared pan. Place pan into air fryer. Bake 10 minutes or until golden brown.

3 In a large bowl, mix remaining 1/2 cup butter, remaining 1/2 cup brown sugar, maple syrup, heavy whipping cream, and vanilla until well combined. Stir in pecans and salt. Place mixture in baked crust.

4 Place pan into air fryer basket. Bake 15 minutes or until top is smooth and a knife inserted into the center comes out clean. Let cool 1 hour before serving.

PER SERVING

CALORIES: 496 | FAT: 34g | SODIUM: 301mg | CARBOHYDRATES: 43g | FIBER: 2g | SUGAR: 30g | PROTEIN: 3g

Chocolate Chip Banana Blondies

Banana bread lovers, this one is for you. These blondies have all the best flavors of the bread in a chewy bar. And like all great banana breads, these dense bars are loaded with tasty chocolate chips, making them rich and extra delicious.

Hands-on time: 10 minutes
Cook time: 30 minutes

Serves 9

2 large ripe bananas, peeled
$3/4$ cup granulated sugar
$1/4$ cup light brown sugar, packed
$1/2$ cup salted butter, softened
1 teaspoon vanilla extract
1 cup all-purpose flour
$1/2$ cup semisweet chocolate chips

1 Preheat air fryer to 320°F. Spray an 8" × 8" baking pan with cooking spray.

2 In a large bowl, mash bananas until mostly smooth. Stir in granulated sugar, brown sugar, butter, and vanilla until well combined.

3 Stir in flour until just combined, then fold in chocolate chips. Place batter in prepared pan.

4 Place pan into air fryer basket. Bake 30 minutes or until golden brown and a toothpick inserted into the center comes out clean. Let cool at least 2 hours before serving.

PER SERVING

CALORIES: 301 | **FAT:** 13g | **SODIUM:** 84mg | **CARBOHYDRATES:** 46g | **FIBER:** 2g | **SUGAR:** 31g | **PROTEIN:** 2g

Frosted Gingerbread Bars

What's better than gingerbread with regular frosting? Gingerbread with cream cheese frosting. These chewy bars covered in fluffy cream cheese frosting have all the flavor and cheer of gingerbread cookies.

Hands-on time: 11 minutes
Cook time: 15 minutes

Serves 12

- 1/2 cup white chocolate chips
- 1/4 cup plus 2 tablespoons salted butter, divided
- 3/4 cup light brown sugar, packed
- 2 tablespoons molasses
- 1 teaspoon vanilla extract
- 1 teaspoon ground cinnamon
- 1 teaspoon ground ginger
- 1/4 teaspoon ground nutmeg
- 1/4 teaspoon ground allspice
- 1 cup all-purpose flour
- 2 large eggs
- 4 ounces cream cheese, softened
- 2 cups confectioners' sugar
- 1 tablespoon whole milk

ADD COLOR!

Make these bars festive by adding colorful sprinkles to fit whatever theme you're looking for. You can also add sparkling sugar for a glittery, snow-like effect.

1. Preheat air fryer to 320°F. Spray an 8" × 8" baking pan with cooking spray.

2. In a medium microwave-safe bowl, melt white chocolate chips and 1/4 cup butter by microwaving in 30-second increments, stirring between each cook time until mixture is smooth, about 1 minute.

3. Add brown sugar, molasses, and vanilla to white chocolate mixture and stir.

4. Add cinnamon, ginger, nutmeg, allspice, and flour, stirring until well combined.

5. Stir in eggs until just combined, then place mixture in prepared pan.

6. Place pan into air fryer basket. Bake 15 minutes or until edges are set and a toothpick inserted into the center comes out clean. Let cool 1 hour.

7. To make the frosting, use a handheld electric mixer to whip cream cheese, remaining 2 tablespoons butter, and confectioners' sugar in a large bowl until smooth. Add milk and stir. The frosting should spread easily but not be overly soft and runny. Spread frosting over top of bars, then slice and serve.

PER SERVING

CALORIES: 301 | FAT: 11g | SODIUM: 104mg | CARBOHYDRATES: 46g | FIBER: 0g | SUGAR: 37g | PROTEIN: 3g

Strawberry Oatmeal Bars

Oatmeal is one of the easiest breakfasts to prepare, but it can sometimes feel monotonous. These easy-to-make bars are a great way to meal prep and are sure to brighten your morning. The secret? Freeze-dried strawberries! They give the bars that classic strawberry flavor you might recognize from the packages of microwavable instant oatmeal. They're often found near the dried fruit section in grocery stores.

Hands-on time: 10 minutes

Cook time: 8 minutes

Serves 9

1 ounce freeze-dried strawberries

¼ cup all-purpose flour

¼ cup old-fashioned oats

¼ cup instant oats

⅓ cup granulated sugar

2 tablespoons light brown sugar, packed

6 tablespoons salted butter, melted

1 large egg

¼ cup whole milk

1 Preheat air fryer to 320°F. Spray an 8" × 8" baking pan with cooking spray.

2 Place freeze-dried strawberries into a food processor and process 10 seconds or until pieces are broken down into a fine powder.

3 Place powder in a medium bowl and mix with flour, old-fashioned oats, instant oats, granulated sugar, and brown sugar until well combined. Mix in butter, egg, and milk until well combined. Place batter into prepared pan.

4 Place pan into air fryer basket. Bake 8 minutes or until top is golden brown and a toothpick inserted into the center comes out clean. Let cool 1 hour before slicing and serving.

PER SERVING

CALORIES: 163 | FAT: 8g | SODIUM: 72mg | CARBOHYDRATES: 20g | FIBER: 1g | SUGAR: 13g | PROTEIN: 2g

Cinnamon Roll Blondies

All the yummy flavors of a cinnamon roll, in a chewy, flavorful blondie! These bars feature a cinnamon swirl and a creamy glaze. Whether you're having them for breakfast or for a treat, you'll be able to enjoy all the classic flavors without all the hassle of the traditional rolls.

Hands-on time: 15 minutes
Cook time: 30 minutes

Serves 9

1 cup granulated sugar
$\frac{1}{2}$ cup plus 2 tablespoons salted butter, softened, divided
1 tablespoon vanilla extract
2 large eggs
$1\frac{1}{2}$ cups all-purpose flour
$1\frac{1}{2}$ teaspoons baking powder
$\frac{1}{3}$ cup light brown sugar, packed
$\frac{1}{2}$ tablespoon cinnamon
$\frac{1}{2}$ cup confectioners' sugar
1 ounce cream cheese, softened
2 tablespoons heavy whipping cream

1 Preheat air fryer to 300°F. Spray an 8" × 8" baking pan with cooking spray.

2 In a large bowl, mix granulated sugar, $\frac{1}{2}$ cup butter, and vanilla until well combined. Stir in eggs. Add flour and baking powder and stir until well combined. Place mixture in prepared pan.

3 In a small bowl, mix brown sugar, cinnamon, and remaining 2 tablespoons butter. Place spoonfuls of mixture around top of blondie mixture, then use a knife to make swirls in the batter.

4 Place pan into air fryer basket. Bake 30 minutes or until golden brown. Let cool at least 1 hour.

5 To make the glaze, whisk together confectioners' sugar, cream cheese, and heavy whipping cream in a small bowl until smooth, then drizzle over cooled blondies before serving.

PER SERVING

CALORIES: 370 | **FAT:** 15g | **SODIUM:** 213mg | **CARBOHYDRATES:** 53g | **FIBER:** 1g | **SUGAR:** 36g | **PROTEIN:** 4g

S'mores Bars

These bars are sure to be a hit with the family. With a bar version, you can enjoy the taste of the classic summertime dessert year-round. Gooey chocolate and yummy marshmallow cover these bars for a sweet, decadent treat.

Hands-on time: 10 minutes
Cook time: 9 minutes

Serves 9

¼ cup salted butter, melted
½ cup light brown sugar, packed
¼ teaspoon baking powder
¼ teaspoon salt
3 graham cracker sheets, crushed
½ cup all-purpose flour
1 cup semisweet chocolate chips
2 cups mini marshmallows

1 Preheat air fryer to 400°F. Line a 6" round baking pan with parchment.

2 In a medium bowl, mix butter, brown sugar, baking powder, and salt until well combined. Add graham crackers and flour and stir until well combined. Reserve ¼ cup dough. Press remaining dough into bottom of prepared pan.

3 Place pan into air fryer basket. Bake 4 minutes or until crust is golden brown on top. Adjust the temperature to 300°F.

4 Place chocolate chips on crust, then top with marshmallows. Break off pieces from reserved dough and scatter on top of marshmallows.

5 Place pan into air fryer basket. Bake 5 minutes or until marshmallows are golden brown and chocolate is melted. Let cool 15 minutes before serving.

PER SERVING

CALORIES: 269 | FAT: 11g | SODIUM: 154mg | CARBOHYDRATES: 43g | FIBER: 2g | SUGAR: 30g | PROTEIN: 2g

Granola Bars

These Granola Bars are super easy and fun to make. The best part is that you can always add (or substitute) your favorite things to make them your own and suit your taste, such as pepitas, dried fruit, or nuts. These bars are golden and crispy on the outside but have a chewy middle.

Hands-on time: 10 minutes
Cook time: 10 minutes

Serves 8

6 tablespoons salted butter, melted
¼ cup light brown sugar, packed
½ cup honey
½ teaspoon salt
1½ cups old-fashioned oats
1 cup quick oats
½ cup mini chocolate chips
½ cup sweetened shredded coconut
¼ cup chopped pecans

1 Preheat air fryer to 350°F. Spray an 8" × 8" baking dish with cooking spray and line with parchment.

2 In a large bowl, whisk together butter, brown sugar, honey, and salt.

3 Fold in old-fashioned oats and quick oats until well combined, then fold in chocolate chips, coconut, and pecans. Place mixture in prepared dish.

4 Place dish into air fryer basket. Bake 10 minutes or until golden brown. Let cool completely before slicing. The bars will firm up and become crunchy on the edges as they cool.

PER SERVING

CALORIES: 380 | FAT: 17g | SODIUM: 240mg | CARBOHYDRATES: 53g | FIBER: 4g | SUGAR: 32g | PROTEIN: 5g

6

Cakes, Muffins, and Sweet Breads

Cakes go hand in hand with celebrations, and muffins and sweet breads are a regular part of a delicious morning. They all have some similarities, but the best among them is how easy they are to make in your air fryer.

Recommended tools for this chapter include a 6" cake pan, 4" × 9" loaf pan, 6-cup Bundt pan, and silicone baking cups. These are all small, inexpensive pieces of bakeware that will make your air fryer baked goods that much better.

With recipes from Vanilla Sprinkle Cake to Double Chocolate Zucchini Bread, this chapter is full of moist and fluffy confections to make your days sweeter, plus some notes about easy homemade frostings that will take your treats to the next level!

Cream Cheese Pound Cake

Whether you need a weeknight pick-me-up or a celebratory sweet treat, this recipe will rise to the occasion. The air fryer creates a dark golden crust on the top and sides that make the buttery, soft inside stand out even more. Serve with your favorite mixture of berries, fruit syrup, and whipped cream.

Hands-on time: 15 minutes
Cook time: 50 minutes

Serves 12

4 ounces cream cheese, softened
6 tablespoons salted butter
2 cups granulated sugar
1 tablespoon vanilla extract
1 teaspoon almond extract
3 large eggs
1 cup all-purpose flour

1 Preheat air fryer to 300°F. Spray an 8" Bundt pan generously with cooking spray.

2 In a large bowl, use an electric hand mixer to beat cream cheese, butter, and sugar until light and fluffy, about 2 minutes.

3 Add vanilla and almond extract and mix well. Add eggs and mix until well combined, about 2 minutes.

4 Slowly add flour, stirring until just combined. Pour batter in prepared pan.

5 Place pan into air fryer basket. Bake 50 minutes or until dark golden brown on top and a toothpick inserted into the center comes out clean.

6 Let cool 10 minutes in pan, then flip over onto a cutting board or plate before serving.

PER SERVING

CALORIES: 274 | FAT: 9g | SODIUM: 98mg | CARBOHYDRATES: 42g | FIBER: 0g | SUGAR: 34g | PROTEIN: 3g

Lemon Lava Cakes

Lemon may not be the first flavor you think of when you hear "lava cake," but try these out and you'll understand why that shouldn't be the case. These luscious cakes are oozing with silky lemon filling, and the outside is soft with just a hint of crunch.

Hands-on time: 11 minutes
Cook time: 10 minutes

Yields 2, 1 per serving

1/2 cup white chocolate chips
4 tablespoons salted butter
2 large eggs
1 teaspoon vanilla extract
2 medium lemons, zested and juiced
1/4 teaspoon salt
3/4 cup all-purpose flour
1/2 cup confectioners' sugar

1 In a medium microwave-safe bowl, melt white chocolate chips and butter in microwave in 30-second intervals, stirring between each until mixture is completely smooth, about 1 minute. Let cool 5 minutes.

2 Preheat air fryer to 350°F. Spray two 4" ramekins with cooking spray.

3 Add eggs, vanilla, and 2 tablespoons lemon juice and zest to white chocolate mixture until well combined. Whisk in salt, flour, and confectioners' sugar until smooth. Divide batter evenly between ramekins.

4 Place ramekins into air fryer basket. Bake 10 minutes or until cake edges pull away from ramekins and the center jiggles only slightly when tapped. Let cool 5 minutes before serving.

PER SERVING

CALORIES: 786 | FAT: 39g | SODIUM: 582mg | CARBOHYDRATES: 90g | FIBER: 2g | SUGAR: 51g | PROTEIN: 14g

Chocolate Lava Cakes

In just under 20 minutes you can have fresh and delicious lava cakes! These are perfect for any chocolate lover. They don't require many ingredients, and they rival any chocolate lava cakes you may have had before. These decadent cakes go well with fresh fruit, ice cream, or even just a dusting of confectioners' sugar for a pretty presentation.

Hands-on time: 11 minute
Cook time: 7 minutes

Yields 4, 1 per serving

4 large eggs
2 teaspoons vanilla extract
$1/4$ teaspoon salt
6 tablespoons unsalted
　　butter
$1^1/_2$ cups semisweet
　　chocolate chips
$1/2$ cup all-purpose flour

1　Preheat air fryer to 350°F. Spray four 4" ramekins with cooking spray.

2　In a medium bowl, whisk together eggs, vanilla, and salt until well combined.

3　In a medium microwave-safe bowl, melt butter and chocolate chips in 20-second intervals, stirring between each interval until mixture is smooth and fully melted, about 1 minute.

4　Slowly pour in bowl with egg mixture and stir until fully incorporated. Add flour and whisk until completely smooth. The mixture should be easily pourable. Divide batter evenly among ramekins.

5　Place ramekins into air fryer basket. Bake 7 minutes. Let cool 5 minutes, then use a butter knife to loosen sides of cakes from ramekins.

6　To serve, place a small dessert plate upside down on top of each ramekin. Quickly flip ramekin and plate upside down so cake drops to the plate. Let cool 5 minutes, then serve.

PER SERVING

CALORIES: 614 | **FAT:** 40g | **SODIUM:** 226mg | **CARBOHYDRATES:** 56g | **FIBER:** 4g | **SUGAR:** 38g | **PROTEIN:** 11g

Molten Cookie Butter Cakes

This twist on a lava cake has it all: a delicious cookie crunch on the outside and an ultra-creamy, cookie-flavored inside. Cookie butter is made of spiced cookies, most commonly speculoos, ground up and blended with sugar and oil until it's spreadable. It's a dessert version of nut butter and has a unique flavor all its own, which makes these cakes really stand out.

Hands-on time: 10 minutes
Cook time: 8 minutes

Yields 2, 1 per serving

1 large egg
1 large egg yolk
$^1/_2$ cup light brown sugar, packed
1 teaspoon vanilla extract
$^1/_4$ cup cookie butter
$^1/_2$ cup all-purpose flour
$^1/_4$ teaspoon salt

1 Preheat air fryer to 350°F. Spray two 4" ramekins with cooking spray.

2 In a medium bowl, whisk together egg, egg yolk, brown sugar, and vanilla until smooth. Add cookie butter and stir until smooth, then fold in flour and salt until fully combined. Divide batter evenly between ramekins.

3 Place ramekins into the air fryer basket. Bake 8 minutes or until edges are browned and the center is mostly set.

4 Let cool 5 minutes, then use a butter knife to loosen sides of cakes from ramekins.

5 To serve, place a small dessert plate upside down on top of each ramekin. Quickly flip ramekin and plate upside down so cake drops to the plate. Let cool 5 minutes, then serve.

PER SERVING

CALORIES: 561 | FAT: 16g | SODIUM: 410mg | CARBOHYDRATES: 96g | FIBER: 1g | SUGAR: 65g | PROTEIN: 9g

Easy Candy Cookie Cake

This super easy recipe uses cake mix as the base to make a fast cookie cake for a special occasion. Leftover candy from a party or Halloween? This recipe is a great use for it. You can chop up whatever you have and add it to the top for a yummy treat.

Hands-on time: 10 minutes
Cook time: 15 minutes

Serves 8

1 (15.25-ounce) box yellow cake mix
$\frac{1}{2}$ cup salted butter, melted
2 large eggs
$\frac{1}{4}$ cup light brown sugar, packed
$1\frac{1}{4}$ cups candy-coated chocolates, divided
1 (12-ounce) can whipped chocolate frosting

ALUMINUM PAN

If you're planning to take this recipe on the go for a gathering, you can bake it in an 8" round disposable aluminum pan. Keep all the cooking directions the same and just be sure to let it completely cool before covering it to avoid it getting soggy.

1 Preheat air fryer to 320°F. Lightly spray an 8" round baking pan with cooking spray.

2 In a large bowl, whisk together cake mix, butter, eggs, and brown sugar. Add 1 cup candy-coated chocolates and stir to incorporate. Pour batter into prepared pan.

3 Place pan into air fryer basket. Bake 15 minutes or until edges are golden brown and a toothpick inserted into the center comes out clean.

4 Place frosting into a piping bag fitted with a 1M tip and make swirls around edges of cooled cake. Chop remaining $\frac{1}{4}$ cup candies and sprinkle on top of frosting.

PER SERVING

CALORIES: 681 | **FAT:** 31g | **SODIUM:** 561mg | **CARBOHYDRATES:** 92g | **FIBER:** 2g | **SUGAR:** 45g | **PROTEIN:** 6g

Banana Nut Muffins

These muffins are not only easy; they also bake in just 10 minutes. They're soft and fluffy with the perfect amount of crunch from the walnuts. Be sure to use overripe bananas for these muffins for maximum banana flavor.

Hands-on time: 10 minutes
Cook time: 30 minutes

Yields 12, 1 per serving

1 cup all-purpose flour
1 teaspoon baking powder
¼ teaspoon salt
½ teaspoon ground cinnamon
2 large overripe bananas, peeled and mashed
5 tablespoons salted butter, melted
1 large egg
1 teaspoon vanilla extract
½ cup walnuts, chopped

1 Preheat air fryer to 300°F. Spray twelve foil baking liners with cooking spray.

2 In a large bowl, mix flour, baking powder, salt, and cinnamon.

3 In a medium bowl, mix bananas, butter, egg, and vanilla.

4 Pour the wet ingredients into the dry ingredients and stir to combine. Fold in walnuts.

5 Spoon 3 tablespoons batter into each prepared liner.

6 Place liners into air fryer basket, working in batches as needed. Bake 10 minutes or until lightly browned and a toothpick inserted into the center comes out clean. Let cool 5 minutes before serving.

PER SERVING

CALORIES: 137 | FAT: 8g | SODIUM: 133mg | CARBOHYDRATES: 13g | FIBER: 1g | SUGAR: 3g | PROTEIN: 3g

Apple Spice Muffins

These spiced muffins are perfect for fall. They're fragrant, fluffy, and delicious. The green apples offer a hint of tartness. If you prefer a sweeter apple, try Fuji or Honeycrisp.

Hands-on time: 15 minutes
Cook time: 36 minutes

Yields 12, 1 per serving

1 cup all-purpose flour
1/2 cup light brown sugar, packed
1/2 teaspoon baking powder
1/2 teaspoon salt
1/2 cup whole milk
1 large egg
1 teaspoon vanilla extract
1/4 cup salted butter, melted
2 Granny Smith apples, peeled, cored, and chopped
1 teaspoon ground cinnamon
1/4 teaspoon ground nutmeg
1/4 cup granulated sugar

APPLE PIE SPICE

For an extra-flavorful muffin, try swapping the spices in this recipe for 1 teaspoon apple pie spice. It's an easy way to add extra spices if you have it on hand. It's available at most grocery stores.

1 Preheat air fryer to 350°F. Spray twelve foil baking liners with cooking spray.

2 In a large bowl, whisk together flour, brown sugar, baking powder, and salt.

3 Whisk in milk, egg, vanilla, and butter until a smooth batter forms, then fold in apples.

4 Fill prepared liners halfway with batter.

5 In a small bowl, mix cinnamon, nutmeg, and granulated sugar. Sprinkle even amounts mixture on top of each muffin, then swirl in with a toothpick.

6 Place liners into air fryer basket, working in batches. Bake 12 minutes or until edges and tops are golden brown and a toothpick inserted into the center comes out clean. Serve warm.

PER SERVING

CALORIES: 149 | FAT: 4g | SODIUM: 160mg | CARBOHYDRATES: 25g | FIBER: 1g | SUGAR: 16g | PROTEIN: 2g

Lemon Poppy Seed Muffins

This flavor is always a classic, and now it's easier than ever. These golden brown muffins are bright, fluffy, and perfectly sweetened. If you don't enjoy poppy seeds, feel free to omit them. The lemon is the real star of the show here.

Hands-on time: 10 minutes
Cook time: 15 minutes

Yields 12, 1 per serving

1 cup all-purpose flour
1/2 cup granulated sugar
1 teaspoon baking powder
1/4 cup salted butter, melted
1 large egg
1/2 cup whole milk
1 medium lemon, zested and juiced
1 tablespoon poppy seeds

1 Preheat air fryer to 300°F. Spray twelve foil baking liners with cooking spray.

2 In a medium bowl, whisk together flour, sugar, and baking powder.

3 In a separate medium bowl, mix butter, egg, milk, and lemon zest and juice.

4 Add the wet ingredients to the dry ingredients and stir until just combined. Fold in poppy seeds.

5 Fill prepared liners halfway with batter.

6 Place liners into air fryer basket, working in batches as needed. Bake 15 minutes or until edges are browned. Let cool 10 minutes before serving.

PER SERVING

CALORIES: 120 | FAT: 5g | SODIUM: 81mg | CARBOHYDRATES: 17g | FIBER: 0g | SUGAR: 9g | PROTEIN: 2g

Pumpkin Muffins

These spiced muffins are a great option for flavorful and fun meal prepping! You'll love making a batch of these and enjoying them all week long. These delicious muffins are perfect with coffee for breakfast, or you can enjoy one as an afternoon pick-me-up.

Hands-on time: 10 minutes
Cook time: 15 minutes

Yields 12, 1 per serving

- ½ cup salted butter, softened
- 1 cup light brown sugar, packed
- 1 teaspoon vanilla extract
- 2 large eggs
- ½ cup pumpkin purée
- 1½ teaspoons pumpkin pie spice
- 1½ teaspoons ground cinnamon
- ½ teaspoon salt
- 1½ teaspoons baking powder
- 1½ cups all-purpose flour

1. Preheat air fryer to 350°F. Spray twelve foil baking liners with cooking spray.

2. In a large bowl, use an electric hand mixer to beat butter, brown sugar, and vanilla until fluffy, about 3 minutes. Mix in eggs, pumpkin purée, pumpkin pie spice, cinnamon, and salt until well combined.

3. In a medium bowl, whisk together baking powder and flour. Slowly add flour mixture to the wet ingredients, stirring until just combined.

4. Fill each prepared liner halfway with batter.

5. Place liners into air fryer basket, working in batches as needed. Bake 15 minutes or until golden brown and a toothpick inserted into the center comes out clean. Serve warm.

PER SERVING

CALORIES: 213 | **FAT:** 8g | **SODIUM:** 236mg | **CARBOHYDRATES:** 31g | **FIBER:** 1g | **SUGAR:** 18g | **PROTEIN:** 3g

Gingerbread Muffins

These unsuspecting muffins are packed with holiday flavors, and they're perfect for breakfast!

Hands-on time: 10 minutes
Cook time: 12 minutes

Yields 12, 1 per serving

1 cup all-purpose flour
1/2 cup light brown sugar, packed
1/2 teaspoon baking powder
1/2 teaspoon salt
2 tablespoons molasses
1/4 cup whole milk
1 large egg
1 teaspoon vanilla extract
1/2 tablespoon ground cinnamon
1 1/2 teaspoons ground ginger
1/4 teaspoon ground cloves

1 Preheat air fryer to 320°F. Spray twelve foil baking liners with cooking spray.

2 In a large bowl, mix all ingredients until well combined into a smooth batter.

3 Fill each prepared liner halfway with batter.

4 Place liners into air fryer basket, working in batches as needed. Bake 12 minutes or until a toothpick inserted into the center comes out clean. Serve warm.

PER SERVING

CALORIES: 94 | FAT: 0g | SODIUM: 129mg | CARBOHYDRATES: 20g | FIBER: 1g | SUGAR: 12g | PROTEIN: 2g

Cherry Pineapple Dump Cake

Dump cakes are a super easy way to make a tasty and flavorful dessert with little effort. This recipe turns a boxed cake mix into a crumble that bakes to a beautiful golden brown.

Hands-on time: 5 minutes
Cook time: 20 minutes

Serves 6, 1/2 cup per serving

1 cup canned crushed pineapple with juice
1 cup cherry pie filling
1 cup yellow boxed cake mix
1/4 cup salted butter, cubed

1 Preheat air fryer to 320°F. Spray a 6" round baking pan with cooking spray.

2 Place pineapple in bottom of prepared pan, then top evenly with pie filling.

3 Place cake mix and butter into a food processor. Pulse ten times or until texture is similar to coarse sand. Sprinkle mix on top of pie filling, pressing some pieces together to make dime-sized chunks.

4 Place pan into air fryer basket. Bake 20 minutes or until top is golden brown. Cool before serving.

PER SERVING

CALORIES: 247 | FAT: 10g | SODIUM: 229mg | CARBOHYDRATES: 38g | FIBER: 1g | SUGAR: 6g | PROTEIN: 1g

Chocolate Cupcakes

This recipe is a staple! These cupcakes are super moist thanks to the buttermilk. They have just a bit of tang, which makes the chocolate flavor all the more appetizing. Plus, the coffee adds a depth of flavor that's so much more delicious than just the typical chocolate cupcakes. If you do need to skip the coffee though, feel free to swap with equal parts water or milk.

Hands-on time: 10 minutes
Cook time: 10 minutes

Yields 16, 1 per serving

1 cup all-purpose flour
1/2 cup granulated sugar
1/2 cup light brown sugar, packed
1/3 cup unsweetened cocoa powder
1 teaspoon baking soda
1/2 teaspoon salt
1 large egg
1/2 cup buttermilk
1/2 cup vegetable oil
1 teaspoon vanilla extract
1/2 cup brewed hot coffee

1 Preheat air fryer to 325°F. Spray sixteen foil baking liners with cooking spray.

2 In a large bowl, whisk together flour, granulated sugar, brown sugar, cocoa powder, baking soda, and salt until combined.

3 Add egg, buttermilk, oil, vanilla, and coffee, then stir until well combined. The batter will be thin.

4 Fill prepared liners halfway with batter.

5 Place liners into air fryer basket, working in batches as needed. Bake 10 minutes or until the centers are firm and a toothpick inserted into the center comes out clean. Serve warm.

PER SERVING

CALORIES: 154 | FAT: 7g | SODIUM: 166mg | CARBOHYDRATES: 20g | FIBER: 1g | SUGAR: 13g | PROTEIN: 2g

Cranberry Upside-Down Cake

This spin on pineapple upside-down cake is super delicious and perfect for fall when fresh cranberries are abundant in stores. The tart cranberry and warm spices pair perfectly together for a scrumptious treat.

Hands-on time: 15 minutes
Cook time: 35 minutes

Serves 6

- 1/3 cup plus 2 tablespoons salted butter, softened, divided
- 1/4 cup light brown sugar, packed
- 1 tablespoon heavy whipping cream
- 3/4 cup all-purpose flour
- 1/2 cup granulated sugar
- 2 teaspoons baking powder
- 1/4 cup sour cream
- 1/4 cup whole milk
- 1 tablespoon orange zest
- 1 teaspoon vanilla extract
- 1/2 teaspoon ground cinnamon
- 1/4 teaspoon ground cloves
- 1 cup cranberries

1 In a small saucepan over medium heat, melt 2 tablespoons butter, about 1 minute. Add brown sugar and heavy whipping cream and continue to cook and stir frequently until mixture begins to thicken and bubble, about 10 minutes, then pour in a small bowl.

2 Preheat air fryer to 320°F. Spray a 6" round cake pan with cooking spray.

3 In a medium bowl, mix remaining 1/3 cup butter, flour, granulated sugar, baking powder, sour cream, milk, and orange zest until smooth. Stir in vanilla, cinnamon, and cloves until well combined.

4 Pour brown sugar mixture in prepared baking pan. Add cranberries on top in an even layer. Pour cake batter on top of cranberries and smooth into an even layer.

5 Place pan into air fryer basket. Bake 25 minutes or until edges are browned and a toothpick inserted into the center comes out clean.

6 Let cool 15 minutes. Place an 8" plate upside down on top of pan and flip upside down to remove cake. Serve warm.

PER SERVING

CALORIES: 325 | FAT: 16g | SODIUM: 286mg | CARBOHYDRATES: 41g | FIBER: 1g | SUGAR: 27g | PROTEIN: 2g

Flourless Chocolate Cake

This fudgy yet delicate cake is perfect for any occasion. If you love fudgy brownies, you will be making this cake over and over again. Each slice is dense and rich. Serve this cake with a dusting of confectioners' sugar for a beautiful presentation.

Hands-on time: 11 minutes
Cook time: 30 minutes

Serves 8

1 cup semisweet chocolate chips
1/4 cup salted butter
1 large egg
1 large egg yolk
1 teaspoon vanilla extract
1/2 cup granulated sugar
1/4 cup unsweetened cocoa powder
1/2 teaspoon salt
1 teaspoon instant espresso powder
1/4 cup confectioners' sugar

1. Preheat air fryer to 350°F. Spray a 6" baking pan with cooking spray.

2. In a medium microwave-safe bowl, melt chocolate chips and butter in microwave in 30-second intervals, stirring between each until mixture is fully melted and smooth, about 1 minute. Stir in egg, egg yolk, and vanilla until fully incorporated.

3. In a separate medium bowl, whisk together sugar, cocoa powder, salt, and espresso powder.

4. Add the dry ingredients to the wet ingredients and stir until well combined and smooth. Pour batter in prepared pan.

5. Place pan into air fryer basket. Bake 30 minutes or until edges gently pull away from sides of pan and a toothpick inserted into the center comes out clean.

6. Let cool 15 minutes, then run a knife along edge of cake. Place an 8" plate upside down on top of pan and flip cake pan upside down onto plate. Remove pan and dust cake with confectioners' sugar before serving.

PER SERVING

CALORIES: 244 | FAT: 13g | SODIUM: 203mg | CARBOHYDRATES: 32g | FIBER: 2g | SUGAR: 28g | PROTEIN: 3g

Vanilla Sprinkle Cake

Some days call for a surprise celebration. This recipe is great to make for those days when you need something special at the last minute. This fluffy cake is loaded with colorful sprinkles, as well as flavor. Top it with your favorite homemade frosting, or even a can of whipped frosting from the store, to make it even sweeter.

Hands-on time: 15 minutes
Cook time: 20 minutes

Serves 6

½ cup all-purpose flour
6 tablespoons granulated sugar
½ teaspoon baking powder
¼ teaspoon salt
¼ cup whole milk
2 tablespoons vegetable oil
1 tablespoon vanilla extract
1 large egg
2 tablespoons rainbow sprinkles

1 Preheat air fryer to 320°F. Cut a piece of parchment and line the bottom of a 6" round baking pan.

2 In a medium bowl, mix flour, sugar, baking powder, and salt until combined.

3 Pour in milk, oil, and vanilla and stir. Add egg and whisk mixture to combine. Gently fold in sprinkles.

4 Pour batter in prepared pan.

5 Place pan into air fryer basket. Bake 20 minutes or until edges and top are browned and a toothpick inserted into the center comes out clean. Let cool 10 minutes before serving.

PER SERVING

CALORIES: 166 | FAT: 6g | SODIUM: 153mg | CARBOHYDRATES: 25g | FIBER: 0g | SUGAR: 17g | PROTEIN: 2g

Mini Pineapple Upside-Down Cakes

These mini cakes are super easy to make and take less than 30 minutes, but the way they look will make it seem as though you've been baking all day. They feature tasty pineapple and a caramelized topping that is sure to impress.

Hands-on time: 10 minutes
Cook time: 15 minutes

Yields 4, 1 per serving

- 2 tablespoons salted butter, melted
- 4 teaspoons light brown sugar, packed
- 4 canned pineapple rings
- 4 maraschino cherries
- $3/4$ cup all-purpose flour
- $1/2$ cup plus 2 tablespoons confectioners' sugar
- $1/2$ teaspoon baking powder
- 1 teaspoon vanilla extract
- $1/2$ cup whole milk
- 2 large eggs

1 Preheat air fryer to 300°F. Spray four 4" ramekins with cooking spray.

2 Pour $1/2$ tablespoon butter into each ramekin and sprinkle with 1 teaspoon brown sugar.

3 Place 1 pineapple ring into each ramekin and place 1 cherry in the center of ring.

4 In a medium bowl, whisk together flour, confectioners' sugar, baking powder, vanilla, milk, and eggs. Distribute batter evenly among ramekins.

5 Place ramekins into air fryer basket and bake 15 minutes or until edges are firm and a toothpick inserted into the center comes out clean.

6 Let cool 10 minutes, then run a knife along cake edges in each ramekin. Place a small plate upside down on top of a ramekin and carefully flip to turn the cake upside down and invert it onto plate; repeat with remaining ramekins. Serve warm.

PER SERVING

CALORIES: 356 | **FAT:** 9g | **SODIUM:** 159mg | **CARBOHYDRATES:** 62g | **FIBER:** 1g | **SUGAR:** 42g | **PROTEIN:** 7g

Carrot Cake Cupcakes

These cupcakes are always a hit and come together easily. They bake in just 10 minutes into warm, spiced, fluffy treats. You'll have a hard time deciding what you love more: the moist base or the sweet cream cheese frosting.

Hands-on time: 15 minutes
Cook time: 10 minutes

Yields 12, 1 per serving

- 1/2 cup salted butter, melted
- 1 cup light brown sugar, packed
- 1 teaspoon vanilla extract
- 2 large eggs
- 1/2 cup whole milk
- 1/4 teaspoon ground cloves
- 1 1/2 teaspoons ground ginger
- 1 tablespoon ground cinnamon
- 1/4 teaspoon ground nutmeg
- 1/2 teaspoon salt
- 2 teaspoons baking powder
- 1 1/2 cups all-purpose flour
- 2 cups grated fresh carrots
- 1/2 cup chopped walnuts
- 8 ounces cream cheese, softened
- 6 tablespoons unsalted butter, softened
- 3 cups confectioners' sugar

FRESH CARROTS

Be sure to use freshly grated carrots for this recipe if at all possible. Freshly grated carrots are softer and have a much better flavor than pre-grated carrots, which will often stay firmer during baking.

1 Preheat air fryer to 325°F. Spray twelve foil baking liners with cooking spray.

2 In a large bowl, mix all ingredients except cream cheese, unsalted butter, and confectioners' sugar until well combined, then fill each prepared liner halfway with batter.

3 Place liners into air fryer basket, working in batches as needed. Bake 10 minutes or until edges are browned and a toothpick inserted into the center comes out clean. Let cool completely, about 15 minutes, before frosting.

4 To make the frosting, whip cream cheese and butter in a large bowl until smooth. Slowly add confectioners' sugar, whipping until fully combined and fluffy. Fill a piping bag fitted with a 1M tip and swirl frosting on top of cupcakes, then serve.

PER SERVING

CALORIES: 468 | FAT: 22g | SODIUM: 343mg | CARBOHYDRATES: 60g | FIBER: 1g | SUGAR: 45g | PROTEIN: 5g

Blueberry Coffee Cakes

These bakery-style treats are fully loaded—from the moist cake to a creamy drizzle on top that will remind you of a streusel. There's enough here to serve at brunch with a group, or make it for yourself and have a slice for breakfast all week long.

Hands-on time: 15 minutes
Cook time: 20 minutes

Serves 12

10 tablespoons salted butter, melted, divided
3/4 cup light brown sugar, packed
1 teaspoon vanilla extract
2 large eggs
3/4 cup whole milk
1/4 teaspoon salt
2 teaspoons baking powder
1 tablespoon lemon zest
1 1/2 cups plus 2 tablespoons all-purpose flour, divided
1 cup blueberries
1/3 cup granulated sugar
1/2 cup confectioners' sugar
1 tablespoon lemon juice

1 Preheat air fryer to 320°F. Spray two 6" round cake pans with cooking spray.

2 In a large bowl, use an electric hand mixer to mix 6 tablespoons butter and brown sugar until fluffy, about 2 minutes.

3 Add vanilla and eggs, then mix until well combined. Pour in milk and mix until smooth. Add salt, baking powder, lemon zest, and 1 1/2 cups flour and mix until smooth. Fold in blueberries.

4 Pour equal amounts batter in prepared pans.

5 To make the crumb topping, combine remaining 4 tablespoons butter, remaining 2 tablespoons flour, and granulated sugar in a small bowl. Use a fork to mix until a wet sand-like consistency forms. There should be a mixture of smaller pieces and some larger dime-sized pieces for an extra-crunchy topping.

6 Sprinkle equal amounts crumb topping on batter, pressing down gently.

7 Place pans into air fryer basket, working in batches as needed. Bake 20 minutes or until topping is browned and a toothpick inserted into the center comes out clean. Let cool for 5 minutes.

8 To make the drizzle, whisk together confectioners' sugar and lemon juice until smooth. Pour over cakes. Serve warm.

PER SERVING

CALORIES: 266 | **FAT:** 10g | **SODIUM:** 228mg | **CARBOHYDRATES:** 39g | **FIBER:** 1g | **SUGAR:** 25g | **PROTEIN:** 4g

Spice Cake

This classic Spice Cake is a hit on any occasion because it's a simple recipe that is loaded with flavor. The cake is moist and not overly sweet, which makes it perfect for enjoying on its own for a subtle dessert, or it can be topped with cream cheese frosting for something a little sweeter.

Hands-on time: 10 minutes
Cook time: 40 minutes

Serves 12

½ cup salted butter, melted
1 cup light brown sugar, packed
1 teaspoon vanilla extract
2 large eggs
½ cup whole milk
⅛ teaspoon ground allspice
¼ teaspoon ground cloves
1 tablespoon ground cinnamon
1½ teaspoons ground ginger
¼ teaspoon ground nutmeg
½ teaspoon salt
1 tablespoon baking powder
1½ cups all-purpose flour
1 cup pecans, chopped

1   Preheat air fryer to 320°F. Spray two 6" round baking pans with cooking spray.

2   In a large bowl, mix butter, brown sugar, and vanilla.

3   Mix remaining ingredients until fully combined into a pourable batter.

4   Distribute batter evenly between prepared pans.

5   Place pans into air fryer basket, working in batches as needed. Bake 20 minutes or until golden brown and a toothpick inserted into the center comes out clean. Serve warm.

PER SERVING

CALORIES: 279 | FAT: 15g | SODIUM: 301mg | CARBOHYDRATES: 33g | FIBER: 2g | SUGAR: 19g | PROTEIN: 4g

FROSTING CHOICES

For this cake, a white or cream cheese frosting would be perfect. You can use a premade can of frosting or easily make your own. To make cream cheese frosting, simply whip together 4 ounces softened cream cheese, 4 tablespoons softened butter, and 4 cups confectioners' sugar until fluffy and smooth.

Eggnog Cake

If you're a fan of eggnog, you'll love this cake. You may not think of eggnog as something to bake with, but it lends flavor and creaminess to cake batter. The extra spices give it a delicious boost and make a moist yet dense and festive cake that you'll keep coming back to.

Hands-on time: 11 minutes
Cook time: 30 minutes

Serves 8

- ¼ cup salted butter, softened
- ¼ cup granulated sugar
- ¼ cup light brown sugar, packed
- 1 large egg
- 1 large egg yolk
- ½ cup plus 2 tablespoons eggnog, divided
- 1 cup all-purpose flour
- 1½ teaspoons baking powder
- ½ teaspoon salt
- ½ teaspoon ground nutmeg
- ¼ cup white chocolate chips

FLAVORED EGGNOG

This recipe calls for classic eggnog, which works great. But if you're in the mood to go outside the box, try a flavored eggnog. You can try pumpkin eggnog for a yummy fall twist! The white chocolate ganache featured here would be an excellent pairing with pumpkin flavor.

1 Preheat air fryer to 350°F. Spray a 6" round cake pan with cooking spray.

2 In a large bowl, use an electric hand mixer to mix butter, granulated sugar, and brown sugar until fluffy, about 2 minutes. Mix in egg and egg yolk until smooth. Stir in ½ cup eggnog.

3 In a separate large bowl, whisk together flour, baking powder, salt, and nutmeg.

4 Pour the wet ingredients into the dry ingredients and mix until well combined. Pour batter into prepared pan.

5 Place pan into air fryer basket. Bake 30 minutes or until golden brown and a toothpick inserted into the center comes out clean. Let cool 30 minutes.

6 To make the ganache, melt white chocolate chips and remaining 2 tablespoons eggnog in a small microwave-safe bowl in 20-second intervals. Stir between each interval until mixture is completely melted and smooth, about 1 minute. Pour over cooled cake before serving.

PER SERVING

CALORIES: 220 | FAT: 9g | SODIUM: 309mg | CARBOHYDRATES: 30g | FIBER: 0g | SUGAR: 18g | PROTEIN: 4g

Coconut Cake

This cake is ultra-moist and loaded with coconut flavor. It's ready in about 30 minutes, making it a great option for any day of the week, and a great option for when you might have impromptu guests. Try it with a vanilla frosting or a layer of whipped topping for a lighter treat.

Hands-on time: 10 minutes
Cook time: 20 minutes

Serves 6

- 1/3 cup salted butter, softened
- 1/2 cup granulated sugar
- 1 teaspoon vanilla extract
- 1 large egg
- 1/2 cup full-fat canned coconut milk
- 1/4 cup sweetened shredded coconut
- 3/4 cup all-purpose flour
- 2 teaspoons baking powder
- 1/4 teaspoon salt

1 Preheat air fryer to 320°F. Spray a 6" round cake dish with cooking spray.

2 In a large bowl, use an electric handheld mixer to mix butter, sugar, and vanilla until smooth, about 2 minutes. Add egg and coconut milk and mix until well combined. Add shredded coconut, flour, baking powder, and salt and mix until smooth.

3 Pour batter in prepared dish.

4 Place dish into air fryer basket. Bake 20 minutes or until top is golden brown and a toothpick inserted into the center comes out clean. Serve warm.

PER SERVING

CALORIES: 279 | **FAT:** 15g | **SODIUM:** 364mg | **CARBOHYDRATES:** 32g | **FIBER:** 1g | **SUGAR:** 18g | **PROTEIN:** 3g

Coffee Cakes

These cakes have a subtle sweetness, which makes them perfect for breakfast and dessert alike. The sponge cake base is topped with cinnamon crumb topping, providing a big crunch. While coffee cake doesn't contain coffee, it tastes delicious alongside a freshly brewed cup.

Hands-on time: 15 minutes
Cook time: 20 minutes

Serves 12

10 tablespoons salted butter, melted, divided
1 cup light brown sugar, packed, divided
1 teaspoon vanilla extract
2 large eggs
3/4 cup whole milk
1/4 teaspoon salt
2 teaspoons baking powder
2 cups all-purpose flour, divided
2 teaspoons ground cinnamon

1   Preheat air fryer to 320°F. Spray two 6" round cake pans with cooking spray.

2   In a large bowl, use an electric hand mixer to mix 6 tablespoons butter and 3/4 cup brown sugar until fluffy, about 2 minutes.

3   Add vanilla and eggs, then mix until well combined. Pour in milk and mix until smooth. Add salt, baking powder, and 1 1/2 cups flour and mix until smooth.

4   Pour equal amounts batter in prepared pans.

5   To make the crumb topping, combine remaining 4 tablespoons butter, remaining 1/4 cup brown sugar, and remaining 1/2 cup flour in a small bowl. Use a fork to mix until a wet sand-like consistency forms. There should be a mixture of smaller pieces and some larger dime-sized pieces for an extra-crunchy topping.

6   Sprinkle equal amounts crumb topping on batter, pressing down gently.

7   Place pans into air fryer basket, working in batches as needed. Bake 20 minutes or until topping is browned and a toothpick inserted into the center comes out clean. Serve warm.

PER SERVING

CALORIES: 256 | FAT: 10g | SODIUM: 229mg | CARBOHYDRATES: 36g | FIBER: 1g | SUGAR: 19g | PROTEIN: 4g

Banana Oatmeal Mini Cakes

This gluten-free cake is perfect for dessert or even breakfast. You can easily scale down this recipe by cutting everything in half or even a quarter for a single serving. These cakes are so fluffy and sweet, you'll forget you're eating oats. Feel free to customize with 1 tablespoon of chopped nuts or a drizzle of peanut butter.

Hands-on time: 10 minutes
Cook time: 15 minutes

Yields 4, 1 per serving

- 2 cups gluten-free rolled oats
- 4 large bananas, peeled
- 4 large eggs
- 4 tablespoons light brown sugar, packed
- 1 teaspoon vanilla extract
- 1 teaspoon baking powder
- ¼ teaspoon salt

1   Preheat air fryer to 350°F. Spray four 4" ramekins with cooking spray.

2   Place all ingredients into a food processor and process 45 seconds or until completely smooth.

3   Pour equal amounts mixture in prepared ramekins.

4   Place ramekins into air fryer basket. Bake 15 minutes or until tops are golden brown and a toothpick inserted into the center comes out clean. Serve warm.

PER SERVING

CALORIES: 422 | FAT: 8g | SODIUM: 342mg | CARBOHYDRATES: 73g | FIBER: 8g | SUGAR: 29g | PROTEIN: 15g

Double Chocolate Zucchini Bread

This bread is perfect for any time of day. It has a dose of vegetables, but you can't even taste it with all the chocolate goodness surrounding it. This recipe is perfect for using up extra zucchini.

Hands-on time: 15 minutes
Cook time: 45 minutes

Serves 12

- 1 cup all-purpose flour
- 1/2 cup unsweetened cocoa powder
- 1/2 cup granulated sugar
- 1/4 cup light brown sugar, packed
- 1 teaspoon baking powder
- 2 large eggs
- 1/3 cup salted butter, melted
- 1 teaspoon vanilla extract
- 1 cup shredded zucchini, excess moisture removed
- 1 cup semisweet chocolate chips

ZUCCHINI'S EXCESS MOISTURE

To remove excess moisture, simply shred the zucchini, then squeeze it in a large kitchen towel or cheesecloth. You may need to shake it a few times, then squeeze again to fully get all the extra moisture out. Too much moisture can cause the batter to be watery.

1 Preheat air fryer to 325°F. Spray a 9" × 4" loaf pan with cooking spray.

2 In a large bowl, whisk together flour, cocoa powder, granulated sugar, brown sugar, and baking powder.

3 In a medium bowl, mix eggs, butter, vanilla, and zucchini.

4 Add the wet ingredients to the dry ingredients, then stir until fully combined. Fold in chocolate chips.

5 Pour batter in prepared pan. Bake 45 minutes or until a knife inserted into the center comes out clean. Let cool at least 30 minutes before serving.

PER SERVING

CALORIES: 228 | **FAT:** 10g | **SODIUM:** 97mg | **CARBOHYDRATES:** 33g | **FIBER:** 3g | **SUGAR:** 21g | **PROTEIN:** 4g

Caramel Monkey Bread Muffins

These mini muffins are a fun dessert that is a spin on regular monkey bread. For this recipe, you'll need to use a stovetop to make a caramel sauce. It's worth the extra effort, which you'll realize when you taste the yummy sauce. Feel free to top the muffins with any remaining sauce.

Hands-on time: 16 minutes
Cook time: 15 minutes

Yields 6, 1 per serving

- 4 tablespoons salted butter, divided
- ¼ cup light brown sugar, packed
- 1½ tablespoons heavy whipping cream
- 8 canned biscuits, quartered to make 32 dough pieces
- ¼ cup granulated sugar
- 2 teaspoons ground cinnamon

1 Preheat air fryer to 350°F. Spray six foil baking liners with cooking spray.

2 To make the caramel sauce, place a small saucepan over medium heat and melt 2 tablespoons butter. When butter is melted, add brown sugar and heavy whipping cream. Continue whisking 2 minutes or until mixture is fragrant, bubbling, and golden brown. Pour into a small bowl.

3 Place remaining 2 tablespoons butter in a medium microwave-safe bowl. Microwave 30 seconds or until melted. Toss quartered biscuits in butter to coat.

4 Place granulated sugar and cinnamon in a large sealable storage bag. Add butter-covered biscuit pieces to bag and shake to coat each piece in mixture.

5 Place five pieces of dough into each prepared liner. Pour 1 tablespoon caramel sauce on top of each serving and tap gently to make sure caramel reaches between all biscuit pieces and to the bottom.

6 Place liners into air fryer basket. Bake 10 minutes or until golden brown and puffy. Let cool 5 minutes, then flip upside down onto a plate to serve, or enjoy with a fork directly from foil liner.

PER SERVING

CALORIES: 351 | FAT: 9g | SODIUM: 793mg | CARBOHYDRATES: 58g | FIBER: 2g | SUGAR: 21g | PROTEIN: 6g

Banana Bread

Who doesn't love a fresh loaf of banana bread? This air fryer version features a crunchy exterior and a tender, moist interior. Each slice is filled with flavor and tastes even better with a little melted butter on top.

Hands-on time: 10 minutes
Cook time: 40 minutes

Serves 12

¼ cup salted butter, melted
2 large ripe bananas, peeled and mashed
½ cup granulated sugar
½ cup light brown sugar, packed
1 large egg
¼ cup sour cream
1 cup all-purpose flour
½ teaspoon baking soda
½ teaspoon salt
1 teaspoon ground cinnamon
½ teaspoon ground nutmeg
½ cup chopped walnuts, divided

1 Preheat air fryer to 325°F. Spray a 4" × 9" loaf pan with cooking spray.

2 In a large bowl, mix butter, bananas, granulated sugar, and brown sugar.

3 Stir in egg and sour cream.

4 In a separate large bowl, whisk together flour, baking soda, salt, cinnamon, and nutmeg.

5 Add the wet ingredients to the dry ingredients and stir to combine. Fold in ¼ cup walnuts.

6 Pour batter in prepared pan and scatter remaining ¼ cup walnuts on top.

7 Bake 40 minutes or until top is golden brown and a toothpick inserted into the center comes out clean. Serve warm.

PER SERVING

CALORIES: 206 | **FAT:** 8g | **SODIUM:** 190mg | **CARBOHYDRATES:** 32g | **FIBER:** 1g | **SUGAR:** 20g | **PROTEIN:** 3g

Cinnamon Swirl Bread

This fluffy, layered sweet bread, made with simple ingredients you likely have on hand, is packed with cinnamon. Try serving it with a pat of butter or even your favorite jam.

Hands-on time: 15 minutes
Cook time: 15 minutes

Serves 12

1 cup all-purpose flour
³/₄ cup granulated sugar, divided
¹/₂ teaspoon baking powder
¹/₂ teaspoon salt
¹/₂ cup whole milk
1 large egg
1 teaspoon vanilla extract
¹/₄ cup salted butter, melted
1 teaspoon ground cinnamon

1 Preheat air fryer to 350°F. Spray a 4" × 9" loaf pan with cooking spray.

2 In a medium bowl, whisk together flour, ¹/₂ cup sugar, baking powder, and salt until well combined. Whisk in milk, egg, vanilla, and butter until smooth.

3 In a small bowl, whisk together cinnamon and remaining ¹/₄ cup sugar.

4 Pour half of the batter into prepared pan, then half of the cinnamon mixture. Repeat with remaining ingredients. Use a knife to swirl topping into batter.

5 Place pan into air fryer basket. Bake 15 minutes or until dark golden brown and a toothpick inserted into the center comes out clean. Serve warm.

PER SERVING

CALORIES: 133 | FAT: 4g | SODIUM: 157mg | CARBOHYDRATES: 21g | FIBER: 0g | SUGAR: 13g | PROTEIN: 2g

7

Biscuits, Savory Breads, and Savory Treats

Baking isn't necessarily all about the sweets. Everyone loves a savory treat that can be enjoyed throughout the day. The air fryer delivers on Buttermilk Biscuits just as well as it does cupcakes. Even yeasted breads are perfect for air fryer baking because the smaller cooking chamber and circulating air make them cook faster than they do in an oven. This is also perfect for when your oven is occupied by the main dish you're cooking, and you want everything to be done at the same time.

From Spinach and Feta–Stuffed Bread to Parmesan Garlic Knots, this chapter's recipes are loaded with flavorful, savory goodies that will make the perfect side dishes and snacks.

Buttermilk Biscuits

These no-fail biscuits come out flaky every time! They're made with simple ingredients, but it's the technique that makes them golden brown and full of buttery goodness. Using frozen grated butter for this recipe is a must because it makes all the difference in texture. You can even throw a stick of butter into the freezer in a sealed freezer-safe bag for up to six months, so it's ready whenever the mood for Buttermilk Biscuits strikes.

Hands-on time: 10 minutes
Cook time: 10 minutes

Yields 8, 1 per serving

1/4 cup salted butter, frozen
2 cups plus 2 tablespoons
   self-rising flour, divided
1/2 teaspoon salt
2/3 cup buttermilk

BISCUIT SHAPE

This recipe makes easy square biscuits. If you'd like to make them circular, feel free to use a round biscuit cutter. However, you should keep in mind you may need to cut out a few and then reroll the dough to continue cutting in order to reach the full yield.

1 Preheat air fryer to 320°F. Cut a piece of parchment to fit air fryer basket.

2 Grate butter into a large bowl. Add 2 cups flour and salt, then mix.

3 Mix in buttermilk and stir gently until a soft dough forms.

4 Dust a clean work surface with remaining 2 tablespoons flour, then turn dough out onto surface. Gently press out into an 8" × 10" rectangle.

5 Use a sharp knife dusted in flour to cut dough into eight squares, then place on parchment.

6 Place parchment into air fryer basket, working in batches as needed. Bake 10 minutes or until golden brown and the center edges feel firm to the touch. Let cool 5 minutes before serving.

PER SERVING

CALORIES: 174 | FAT: 6g | SODIUM: 584mg | CARBOHYDRATES: 24g | FIBER: 1g | SUGAR: 1g | PROTEIN: 4g

Sour Cream and Chive Biscuits

Using fresh herbs can completely change a recipe. They add a bright flavor that can really take a whole meal up a notch. Whether these biscuits are a side dish or the star of a delicious breakfast sandwich, these flavorful biscuits are perfect.

Hands-on time: 10 minutes
Cook time: 20 minutes

Yields 8, 1 per serving

¼ cup salted butter, frozen
2 cups plus 2 tablespoons self-rising flour, divided
½ teaspoon salt
¾ cup sour cream
2 tablespoons chopped fresh chives

1 Preheat air fryer to 320°F. Cut a piece of parchment to fit air fryer basket.

2 Grate butter into a large bowl. Add 2 cups flour and salt, then mix. Add sour cream and mix until well combined.

3 Dust a clean work surface with remaining 2 tablespoons flour, then turn dough out onto surface. Press out into a rectangle. Sprinkle chives over dough, then gently fold dough three times to fully incorporate chives.

4 Gently roll dough out to ¾" thickness. Use a round biscuit cutter to cut out eight circles. Place on parchment 2" apart. You may need to gather dough after cutting a few circles and reroll it to get full yield.

5 Place parchment into air fryer basket, working in batches as needed. Bake 10 minutes or until golden brown. Serve warm.

PER SERVING

CALORIES: 203 | FAT: 9g | SODIUM: 573mg | CARBOHYDRATES: 24g | FIBER: 1g | SUGAR: 1g | PROTEIN: 4g

Jalapeño Cheddar Biscuits

By making these in a drop style instead of using a biscuit cutter, all the little pieces of dough that stick up turn into crunchy golden pieces in the air fryer.

Hands-on time: 10 minutes
Cook time: 16 minutes

Yields 10, 1 per serving

2 cups all-purpose flour
1 tablespoon baking powder
½ teaspoon salt
¼ cup salted butter, melted
¾ cup whole milk
1¼ cups shredded sharp Cheddar cheese, divided
2 tablespoons diced fresh jalapeños

1 Preheat air fryer to 350°F.

2 In a large bowl, mix together flour, baking powder, and salt. Add butter and milk and mix until well combined. Fold in 1 cup Cheddar and jalapeños.

3 Take ¼-cup scoops of dough and place into air fryer basket, working in batches as needed. Top with remaining ¼ cup Cheddar. Bake 8 minutes or until golden brown. Serve warm.

PER SERVING

CALORIES: 200 | FAT: 9g | SODIUM: 300mg | CARBOHYDRATES: 20g | FIBER: 1g | SUGAR: 1g | PROTEIN: 7g

Corn Bread

There's nothing like a yummy side of corn bread. Now you can make this buttery side dish while the main meal finishes up without heating up the whole oven.

Hands-on time: 10 minutes
Cook time: 30 minutes

Serves 6

1 cup all-purpose flour
1 cup cornmeal
⅓ cup granulated sugar
⅓ cup light brown sugar, packed
1 teaspoon salt
1 tablespoon baking powder
1 large egg
1 cup buttermilk
6 tablespoons salted butter, melted

1 Preheat air fryer to 325°F. Spray an 8" × 8" baking dish with cooking spray.

2 In a large bowl, whisk together flour, cornmeal, granulated sugar, brown sugar, salt, and baking powder until well combined. Add egg, buttermilk, and butter and stir until combined.

3 Pour batter into prepared dish. Place dish into air fryer basket. Bake 30 minutes, flipping pan halfway through for even cooking. The corn bread will be done when lightly browned on top and a toothpick inserted into the center comes out mostly clean. Serve warm.

PER SERVING

CALORIES: 378 | FAT: 13g | SODIUM: 787mg | CARBOHYDRATES: 57g | FIBER: 2g | SUGAR: 25g | PROTEIN: 6g

Sweet Cinnamon Biscuits

The air fryer is one of the best ways to make biscuits. While biscuits are normally savory, you can easily whip up a sweet version for dessert. These are a yummy treat by themselves, or they can be enjoyed alongside warm baked fruit.

Hands-on time: 10 minutes
Cook time: 8 minutes

Yields 4, 1 per serving

- 1 cup plus 2 tablespoons all-purpose flour, divided
- 1/4 cup granulated sugar
- 2 teaspoons baking powder
- 1/4 teaspoon salt
- 1 tablespoon ground cinnamon
- 1/2 cup plain full-fat Greek yogurt

1 Preheat air fryer to 350°F.

2 In a large bowl, whisk together 1 cup flour, sugar, baking powder, salt, and cinnamon.

3 Stir in yogurt until a soft dough forms.

4 Dust a clean work surface with remaining 2 tablespoons flour. Section dough into four mounds.

5 Place mounds into air fryer basket. Bake 8 minutes, flipping when 2 minutes remain. Biscuits will be done when golden brown. Serve warm.

PER SERVING

CALORIES: 195 | FAT: 2g | SODIUM: 399mg | CARBOHYDRATES: 40g | FIBER: 2g | SUGAR: 14g | PROTEIN: 6g

Quick Breakfast Bombs

These quick bites are excellent for making ahead and enjoying all week. Each bite has a yummy, cheesy center. They're packed with protein, so you'll have energy. For a sweet take, add 1 tablespoon honey to the melted butter before you brush it over the biscuits.

Hands-on time: 15 minutes
Cook time: 23 minutes

Yields 8, 1 per serving

- ½ pound ground pork sausage
- 2 large eggs
- ¼ teaspoon salt
- ¼ teaspoon ground black pepper
- 2 (7.5-ounce) cans refrigerated biscuits
- ½ cup shredded mild Cheddar cheese
- 2 tablespoons salted butter, melted

1 In a medium skillet over medium heat, brown sausage until no pink remains, about 10 minutes. Drain the fat and return skillet to medium heat.

2 Push sausage to edges of pan, leaving the center clear. Crack eggs into the center of pan and let cook 1 minute.

3 Sprinkle eggs with salt and pepper, then stir into cooked sausage. Continue cooking another 2 minutes or until eggs are fully cooked.

4 Preheat air fryer to 350°F.

5 On a clean work surface, separate biscuits and gently flatten to ½" thickness.

6 Place 1 tablespoon sausage mixture on each of eight biscuits. Sprinkle each with 1 tablespoon cheese.

7 Press edges together, or use a fork, to seal completely. Brush with butter.

8 Place biscuits into air fryer basket, working in batches as needed. Bake 10 minutes, flipping when 3 minutes remain. The biscuits will be golden brown when fully cooked. Serve warm.

PER SERVING

CALORIES: 317 | FAT: 17g | SODIUM: 875mg | CARBOHYDRATES: 27g | FIBER: 2g | SUGAR: 5g | PROTEIN: 11g

Peach Biscuit Bites

Premade dough is a helpful tool for last-minute desserts. It can be sweet or savory, and this recipe takes traditional canned biscuits and sweetens them up for a delicious dessert the whole family can enjoy. The air fryer crisps the biscuits nicely, complementing the soft peaches. A glaze takes this easy recipe to the next level and gives you all the flavors of a cobbler in much less time.

Hands-on time: 10 minutes
Cook time: 14 minutes

Yields 16, 2 per serving

1 (16-ounce) can biscuits, 8 count
1 (15-ounce) can peach slices in water, drained, cut into bite-sized pieces
2 tablespoons salted butter, melted
2 teaspoons ground cinnamon
1/4 cup granulated sugar
1/4 cup confectioners' sugar
2 teaspoons whole milk

1 Preheat air fryer to 350°F. Spray sixteen foil baking liners with cooking spray.

2 Carefully separate each biscuit into two by slowly pulling apart to make sixteen pieces total. Gently press out to flatten each to about 1/4" thickness.

3 Place 1 tablespoon chopped peaches in the center of each biscuit piece.

4 Gather edges of each biscuit together to form around peaches. Press edges together to seal well. Place in prepared liners (with seam side down).

5 Place liners into air fryer basket, working in batches as needed. Bake 7 minutes or until golden brown.

6 Let cool 10 minutes, then carefully remove from liners. Brush each with butter.

7 In a small bowl, mix cinnamon and granulated sugar. Roll each biscuit in mixture, coating on all sides.

8 To make the glaze, whisk confectioners' sugar and milk in a small bowl until smooth and pourable. Drizzle glaze over biscuits before serving.

PER SERVING

CALORIES: 130 | FAT: 4g | SODIUM: 296mg | CARBOHYDRATES: 21g | FIBER: 1g | SUGAR: 8g | PROTEIN: 2g

Focaccia

This bread is one of the best air fryer recipes to keep on hand. You can slice it and use it as a side dish with pasta, turn it into a sandwich, or load it up and make it into a pizza. No matter how you dress it, you'll be amazed at how perfectly this bread bakes in just 10 minutes. Be sure to plan ahead so the dough has time to rise. You can make this up to 12 hours in advance; just cover with plastic wrap and place in the refrigerator after the initial 1-hour rise time, then bring to room temperature before baking.

Hands-on time: 30 minutes
Cook time: 10 minutes

Yields 2

$1^1/_3$ cups hot water, around 110°F

1 tablespoon granulated sugar

$2^1/_2$ teaspoons active dry yeast

$3^1/_2$ cups plus 2 tablespoons bread flour, divided

$^3/_4$ teaspoon salt

$^1/_4$ cup plus 1 tablespoon olive oil, divided

1 In a small bowl, stir water and sugar together. Sprinkle in yeast and gently stir. Let sit 10 minutes or until yeast is foamy.

2 Place $3^1/_2$ cups bread flour and salt in a large bowl, then add yeast mixture and $^1/_4$ cup oil. Use a rubber spatula and stir until well combined.

3 Lightly spray a clean large bowl with cooking spray and place dough in bowl to let rise 1 hour or until doubled in size.

4 Preheat air fryer to 370°F.

5 On a flat, clean work surface dusted with remaining 2 tablespoons flour, separate dough into even halves. Shape each into 8" × 6" rectangles, about $^1/_2$" thick. Press your fingers into the dough to create the classic-looking focaccia dimples. Drizzle with 1 tablespoon oil.

6 Place one dough loaf into air fryer basket, working in batches as needed. Bake 10 minutes, flipping over after 6 minutes. When done, loaf will be golden brown and firm. Serve warm.

PER SERVING

CALORIES: 1,143 | FAT: 29g | SODIUM: 879mg | CARBOHYDRATES: 182g | FIBER: 7g | SUGAR: 7g | PROTEIN: 31g

Parmesan Garlic Knots

You'll be amazed at how dark golden and fluffy the air fryer will make these. These pair well with pasta meals or meatballs.

Hands-on time: 20 minutes
Cook time: 8 minutes

Yields 8, 1 per serving

1⅓ cups hot water, around 110°F

1 tablespoon granulated sugar

2½ teaspoons active dry yeast

3½ cups plus 2 tablespoons bread flour, divided

¾ teaspoon salt

¼ cup plus 1 tablespoon olive oil, divided

1 teaspoon finely minced garlic

3 tablespoons salted butter, melted

1 teaspoon Italian seasoning blend

¼ cup grated Parmesan cheese, divided

1 In a large bowl, stir water and sugar together. Sprinkle in yeast and gently stir mixture. Let sit 10 minutes or until foamy.

2 Place 3½ cups bread flour and salt in a large bowl, then add yeast mixture and ¼ cup oil. Use a rubber spatula and stir until well combined.

3 Lightly spray a clean large bowl with cooking spray and place dough in bowl to let rise 1 hour or until doubled in size.

4 Dust a clean work surface with remaining 2 tablespoons flour then turn out dough and shape into an 8" × 9" rectangle.

5 Using a pizza cutter, slice dough into eight 1"-wide strips. Tie each strip into a knot, then tuck edges under the knot and gently press together to hold its shape. Repeat with remaining strips of dough, then let them rise 15 minutes.

6 Preheat air fryer to 370°F.

7 In a small bowl, mix remaining 1 tablespoon oil, garlic, and butter. Brush mixture over each garlic knot until well coated.

8 Sprinkle Italian seasoning and 2 tablespoons Parmesan over garlic knots.

9 Place garlic knots in air fryer basket. Bake 8 minutes or until knots are golden brown and bounce back from a quick touch.

10 Sprinkle with remaining 2 tablespoons Parmesan and cool 5 minutes before serving.

PER SERVING

CALORIES: 352 | FAT: 14g | SODIUM: 310mg | CARBOHYDRATES: 46g | FIBER: 2g | SUGAR: 2g | PROTEIN: 9g

Ham and Cheese Hand Pies

This flaky meal comes together in no time. These made-from-scratch pies are full of cheesy goodness, and you'll be amazed at how delicious and golden they bake in the air fryer. If you don't like ham, you can use turkey in its place.

Hands-on time: 15 minutes
Cook time: 15 minutes

Yields 4, 1 per serving

1/4 cup salted butter, frozen
2 cups plus 2 tablespoons self-rising flour, divided
2/3 cup whole milk
3/4 cup diced cooked ham
1 cup shredded Cheddar cheese
1 large egg, whisked
1 tablespoon water

EASY SWAPS

If you're low on time, you can skip the process of making the dough. These will turn out just fine with store-bought pie crust from a can in the refrigerated section. Simply omit the ingredients prior to the ham if you choose to skip making the dough yourself.

1. Preheat air fryer to 350°F.

2. Grate butter into a large bowl and whisk with 2 cups flour. Stir in milk until a soft dough forms.

3. Dust a clean work surface with remaining 2 tablespoons flour and turn out dough. Roll dough into a 10" × 12" rectangle, then cut into eight evenly sized rectangles.

4. Place 3 tablespoons ham and 1/4 cup cheese on four rectangles. Top with remaining dough rectangles. Use a fork to press edges together.

5. In a small bowl, whisk together egg and water. Brush mixture over each hand pie.

6. Place hand pies into air fryer basket, working in batches as needed. Bake 15 minutes, flipping after 10 minutes. Pies will be golden brown when done. Serve warm.

PER SERVING

CALORIES: 523 | **FAT:** 24g | **SODIUM:** 1,416mg | **CARBOHYDRATES:** 49g | **FIBER:** 2g | **SUGAR:** 2g | **PROTEIN:** 22g

Soft Pretzels

These pretzels can be topped with your favorite pretzel flavors such as cinnamon and sugar.

Hands-on time: 10 minutes
Cook time: 33 minutes

Yields 6, 1 per serving

2 tablespoons granulated sugar
³/₄ cup whole milk, heated to around 110°F
2¹/₄ teaspoons active dry yeast
¹/₂ teaspoon salt
2 cups plus 4 tablespoons all-purpose flour, divided
¹/₄ cup olive oil
6 cups water
¹/₄ cup baking soda
1 large egg, whisked
2 teaspoons coarse sea salt

MILK SWAP

If you prefer not to use milk, or perhaps realized when going to make this recipe that someone used the last of it, you can substitute the milk with equal amounts of water. The pretzels will have a slightly less rich flavor, but water will get the job done.

1 In a medium bowl, whisk together sugar and milk. Sprinkle in yeast and gently stir. Let sit 5 minutes or until foamy.

2 In a large bowl, add salt, 2 cups flour, and oil, then add yeast mixture. Stir gently until a soft dough forms.

3 Dust a clean work surface with 2 tablespoons flour. Place dough on surface and knead 5 minutes or until dough is smooth.

4 Lightly spray a separate large bowl with cooking spray and place dough in bowl. Cover with plastic wrap and let rise in a warm place until doubled in size.

5 Dust a clean work surface with remaining 2 tablespoons flour. Place dough on surface and cut into six equal pieces. Roll one dough piece into a 15" rope. Form into a pretzel shape by looping the two ends toward the center and twisting, then securing by pressing into the bottom.

6 In a large pot over high heat, boil 6 cups water and add baking soda. Stir to combine.

7 Preheat air fryer to 320°F. Cut two pieces of parchment to fit air fryer basket.

8 Place two pretzels at a time into boiling water for 45 seconds, then place on parchment. Brush with egg and sprinkle with sea salt.

9 Place parchment in air fryer basket. Bake 15 minutes, flipping after 12 minutes. Work in batches. Pretzels will be done when dark golden brown. Transfer to a plate and serve.

PER SERVING

CALORIES: 292 | FAT: 11g | SODIUM: 987mg | CARBOHYDRATES: 39g | FIBER: 2g | SUGAR: 6g | PROTEIN: 8g

Parmesan Herb Biscuits

This easy Italian-inspired side dish is perfect for comfort food! Whether you're enjoying them with a creamy stew or using them to top a casserole, these fluffy biscuits do not disappoint. The key is the buttermilk for extra flavor and a bit of tang that really takes these to the next level.

Hands-on time: 10 minutes
Cook time: 15 minutes

Yields 8, 1 per serving

- 1/3 cup salted butter, frozen
- 2 1/2 cups plus 2 tablespoons self-rising flour, divided
- 1/2 teaspoon salt
- 1/2 cup sour cream
- 1/2 cup buttermilk
- 1/2 cup grated Parmesan cheese
- 1 tablespoon Italian seasoning

1 Preheat air fryer to 320°F. Cut a piece of parchment to fit air fryer basket.

2 Grate butter into a large bowl. Add 2 1/2 cups flour and salt, then mix. Add sour cream and buttermilk and stir gently until a soft dough forms.

3 Fold in Parmesan and Italian seasoning.

4 Dust a clean work surface with remaining 2 tablespoons flour and gently press dough out into an 8" × 10" rectangle.

5 Use a sharp knife dusted in flour to cut dough into eight squares and place on parchment.

6 Place parchment into air fryer basket, working in batches as needed. Bake 15 minutes or until golden brown and the center edges feel firm to the touch. Let cool 5 minutes before serving.

PER SERVING

CALORIES: 269 | FAT: 12g | SODIUM: 807mg | CARBOHYDRATES: 31g | FIBER: 1g | SUGAR: 1g | PROTEIN: 7g

Yeast Dinner Rolls

This classic side bakes beautifully in the air fryer. These rolls develop a dark brown crust and a soft, pillowy textured interior. This is one of those recipes you'll keep on coming back to!

Hands-on time: 30 minutes
Cook time: 15 minutes

Yields 12, 1 per serving

1 cup whole milk
3 tablespoons granulated sugar
2¼ teaspoons active dry yeast
¼ cup unsalted butter, melted
2 large egg yolks
½ teaspoon salt
3 cups plus 2 tablespoons bread flour, divided
¼ cup salted butter, melted

1 Pour milk into a large bowl and whisk in sugar. Add yeast and gently stir. Cover and let sit 10 minutes or until yeast is foamy.

2 Add unsalted butter, egg yolks, salt, and 3 cups flour to yeast mixture. Stir until a soft dough forms.

3 Dust a clean work surface with remaining 2 tablespoons flour and place dough on surface. Knead for 5 minutes or until dough becomes smooth and elastic.

4 Place dough in a clean large bowl and cover with plastic wrap or a clean kitchen towel 2 hours or until doubled in size.

5 Preheat air fryer to 300°F. Spray two 8" × 8" baking pans with cooking spray and line with parchment.

6 Uncover dough and punch down to remove air. Separate dough into twelve pieces and roll into balls. Place six dough balls in each pan, leaving about 3" of space in between. Let rise 30 minutes.

7 Place one pan into air fryer basket. Bake 15 minutes or until golden brown on top. Repeat with the second pan.

8 Brush tops with salted butter and let cool 15 minutes before serving.

PER SERVING

CALORIES: 227 | FAT: 9g | SODIUM: 138mg | CARBOHYDRATES: 29g | FIBER: 1g | SUGAR: 4g | PROTEIN: 6g

Whole-Wheat Dinner Rolls

These rolls are a tasty alternative to regular white rolls. They're a little sweeter from the wheat but are still fluffy in the center. This hearty side has a stronger flavor than regular rolls but goes great with stronger-flavored meals such as stews or roasts.

Hands-on time: 15 minutes
Cook time: 15 minutes

Yields 6, 1 per serving

- ½ cup whole milk
- 2 teaspoons granulated sugar
- 2 teaspoons active dry yeast
- ⅓ cup salted butter, melted
- 1 large egg
- ¼ teaspoon salt
- 1¼ cups whole-wheat flour
- ½ cup plus 2 tablespoons all-purpose flour, divided

HONEY BUTTER

If you have the time to make this topping, you won't regret it. It pairs perfectly with the sweetness of the wheat in these rolls. To make a honey butter glaze, mix equal parts honey and melted butter, then brush over the rolls. Sprinkle with sea salt. It's as simple as that!

1 Pour milk and sugar in a medium bowl and mix. Sprinkle in yeast and gently stir. Let sit 5 minutes or until foamy.

2 In a large bowl, whisk together butter, egg, and salt until well combined, then add yeast mixture, whole-wheat flour, and ½ cup all-purpose flour, and stir until a soft dough forms.

3 Dust a clean work surface with remaining 2 tablespoons all-purpose flour and turn dough out onto surface. Knead dough 10 minutes or until it is smooth and elastic.

4 Spray a clean large bowl with cooking spray and place dough in bowl. Cover with plastic wrap and let rise 2 hours or until doubled in size.

5 Separate dough into six evenly sized pieces and roll into balls. Let rest 45 minutes.

6 Preheat air fryer to 320°F.

7 Place rolls into air fryer basket, working in batches as needed. Bake 15 minutes or until rolls are golden brown and spring back from a quick touch. Let cool 10 minutes before serving.

PER SERVING

CALORIES: 247 | FAT: 11g | SODIUM: 199mg | CARBOHYDRATES: 29g | FIBER: 3g | SUGAR: 3g | PROTEIN: 7g

Pesto Pull-Apart Bread

This bread is full of herbaceous basil pesto and gooey mozzarella. These bites are fluffy and the perfect accompaniment to dinner, but are also perfect for a savory movie night treat. Premade dough makes this recipe super quick and easy.

Hands-on time: 10 minutes
Cook time: 15 minutes

Serves 8

1 (13.8-ounce) tube premade pizza dough
1 cup basil pesto
1½ cups shredded mozzarella cheese, divided
½ cup grated Parmesan cheese
2½ teaspoons Italian seasoning blend, divided

1 Preheat air fryer to 320°F. Spray a 4" × 9" loaf pan with cooking spray.

2 On a clean work surface, press pizza dough out into an 8" × 10" rectangle. Cut lengthwise into three even rectangles.

3 Add ⅓ cup pesto to each rectangle, then top each rectangle with ⅓ cup mozzarella and Parmesan. Sprinkle each rectangle with ½ teaspoon Italian seasoning.

4 Stack the rectangles on top of each other to make a single stack.

5 Carefully cut the stack into 1" slices. Turn the pieces over, so the layers are visible, then place into prepared pan. Sprinkle with remaining mozzarella and remaining Italian seasoning.

6 Place pan into air fryer basket. Bake 15 minutes or until bread is dark golden brown. Check to ensure the very center of the loaf is fully cooked. Let cool at least 10 minutes before serving.

PER SERVING

CALORIES: 315 | **FAT:** 17g | **SODIUM:** 788mg | **CARBOHYDRATES:** 28g | **FIBER:** 1g | **SUGAR:** 4g | **PROTEIN:** 11g

Sun-Dried Tomato and Basil Quick Bread

This easy bread is a great addition to any meal. Whether you're enjoying it as a slice or using it for a delicious turkey sandwich, it's sure to please. The bread has a soft texture with just a little crunch.

Hands-on time: 10 minutes
Cook time: 15 minutes

Serves 12

1 cup all-purpose flour
1/2 teaspoon baking powder
1 large egg
1/2 cup salted butter, melted
3/4 cup whole milk
1/4 cup sun-dried tomatoes, finely chopped
1/2 teaspoon dried basil
1/4 teaspoon dried oregano
1/2 teaspoon salt

1 Preheat air fryer to 320°F. Spray a 4" × 9" loaf pan with cooking spray.

2 In a large bowl, whisk together flour, baking powder, egg, butter, and milk.

3 Fold in tomatoes, basil, oregano, and salt.

4 Place mixture in prepared pan.

5 Place pan into air fryer basket. Bake 15 minutes or until golden brown and a toothpick inserted into the center comes out clean. Let cool 10 minutes before serving.

PER SERVING

CALORIES: 123 | **FAT:** 8g | **SODIUM:** 193mg | **CARBOHYDRATES:** 9g | **FIBER:** 0g | **SUGAR:** 1g | **PROTEIN:** 2g

Mozzarella Biscuit Bites

These bites are a bready take on mozzarella sticks. Instead of a fried bread crumb–coated cheese stick, these use fluffy biscuits to make a delicious cheese-filled bite. They're covered in herbs and grated cheese to add even more flavor.

Hands-on time: 10 minutes
Cook time: 8 minutes

Yields 8, 2 per serving

- 1 (7-ounce) can biscuit dough
- 2 sticks mozzarella string cheese
- 1 large egg
- 1 tablespoon water
- 2 teaspoons Italian seasoning blend
- 3 tablespoons salted butter, melted
- ¼ cup grated Parmesan cheese

1 Preheat air fryer to 400°F.

2 Press each biscuit out to about ¼" thickness. Cut each mozzarella stick into four pieces.

3 Place one mozzarella piece in the center of each biscuit and fold biscuit edges around cheese to completely cover, pinching closed.

4 In a small bowl, whisk together egg and water. Brush each biscuit bite with egg mixture, then sprinkle with seasoning.

5 Place biscuit bites into air fryer basket. Bake 8 minutes or until golden brown.

6 Brush finished bites with butter and sprinkle with Parmesan to serve.

PER SERVING

CALORIES: 157 | **FAT:** 9g | **SODIUM:** 391mg | **CARBOHYDRATES:** 13g | **FIBER:** 1g | **SUGAR:** 2g | **PROTEIN:** 5g

Soda Bread

This classic recipe uses simple ingredients to make a delicious, crusty loaf of bread in no time. The buttermilk gives this bread a unique flavor that's perfect alongside soups and stews. No need to wait for St. Patrick's Day to make it!

Hands-on time: 10 minutes
Cook time: 25 minutes

Serves 8

2 cups plus 2 tablespoons all-purpose flour, divided
3 tablespoons granulated sugar
½ teaspoon baking soda
1½ tablespoons baking powder
¼ teaspoon salt
½ cup salted butter, frozen and grated
¾ cup buttermilk, divided

1 Preheat air fryer to 320°F.

2 In a large bowl, whisk together 2 cups flour, sugar, baking soda, baking powder, and salt until well combined.

3 Stir in grated butter, then pour in ½ cup buttermilk. Stir until just combined.

4 Dust a clean work surface with remaining 2 tablespoons flour. Place dough on surface and shape into a round loaf, about 6" in diameter and 2" high. Brush with remaining ¼ cup buttermilk.

5 Place dough into air fryer basket. Bake 25 minutes or until dark golden brown and a toothpick inserted into the center comes out clean. Let cool at least 30 minutes before serving.

PER SERVING

CALORIES: 248 | **FAT:** 12g | **SODIUM:** 541mg | **CARBOHYDRATES:** 30g | **FIBER:** 1g | **SUGAR:** 6g | **PROTEIN:** 4g

Jalapeño, Bacon, and Cheese Quick Bread

This crunchy bread is packed with spice and savory cheese. It's perfect sliced for the ultimate sandwich, loaded with mayonnaise, deli meats, lettuce, and tomato. Or try it as a breakfast sandwich with a welcome kick. You can't go wrong with this one!

Hands-on time: 10 minutes
Cook time: 15 minutes

Serves 12

1 cup bread flour
1 teaspoon baking powder
$1/2$ cup salted butter, melted
1 large egg
$1/2$ cup cooked crumbled bacon
$1/2$ cup shredded mild Cheddar cheese
$1/4$ cup chopped pickled jalapeños
$1/2$ cup whole milk

1. Preheat air fryer to 320°F. Spray a 4" × 9" loaf pan with cooking spray.

2. In a large bowl, whisk together flour, baking powder, butter, egg, bacon, and Cheddar. Mix in jalapeños.

3. Pour in milk and stir until fully incorporated and a soft batter forms.

4. Pour batter into prepared pan.

5. Place pan into air fryer basket. Bake 15 minutes or until golden brown and a toothpick inserted into the center comes out clean. Let cool at least 10 minutes before serving.

PER SERVING

CALORIES: 176 | FAT: 12g | SODIUM: 318mg | CARBOHYDRATES: 9g | FIBER: 0g | SUGAR: 1g | PROTEIN: 6g

No-Yeast Quick Bagels

These bagels are an air fryer staple. They're firm and fluffy on the inside just like yeast bagels, but take a lot less time and effort. These bagels are perfect for whipping up to bring to brunch, or if you want to make a fast batch on Sunday to enjoy all week long, these will be your new go-to.

Hands-on time: 5 minutes
Cook time: 15 minutes

Yields 6, 1 per serving

2 cups plus 2 tablespoons
   all-purpose flour, divided
1 tablespoon baking powder
$\frac{1}{2}$ teaspoon salt
$1\frac{1}{2}$ cups plain full-fat Greek
   yogurt
1 large egg, whisked

TOAST IT!

Not only can you bake these in the air fryer; you can also toast them! After they're fully cooled, simply slice in half and toast on 400°F for 3–5 minutes until they're your preferred golden color. Spread with cream cheese or your choice of topping and enjoy!

1 In a large bowl, mix 2 cups flour, baking powder, and salt until well combined. Stir in yogurt.

2 Preheat air fryer to 320°F.

3 Dust a clean work surface with remaining 2 tablespoons flour. Turn dough out onto surface and knead 5 minutes or until smooth and elastic.

4 Cut dough into six pieces.

5 Roll each dough piece into an 8"-long rope, then press ends together and form a bagel shape.

6 Brush egg over top of each bagel.

7 Place bagels into air fryer basket. Bake 15 minutes or until golden brown and firm to the touch. Let cool for 15 minutes before slicing.

PER SERVING

CALORIES: 219 | **FAT:** 4g | **SODIUM:** 470mg | **CARBOHYDRATES:** 35g | **FIBER:** 1g | **SUGAR:** 2g | **PROTEIN:** 10g

Spinach Dip Puff Pastry Bites

These bites will be the star of your next gathering. They're very easy to assemble and packed with flavor. Each bite is super flaky and filled with delicious cream cheese. The red pepper flakes really take these to the next level, but if they aren't your thing, feel free to omit.

Hands-on time: 15 minutes
Cook time: 7 minutes

Yields 12, 1 per serving

- 1 (13.2-ounce) package frozen puff pastry, thawed
- 4 ounces cream cheese, softened
- 3/4 cup spinach, chopped
- 2 tablespoons mayonnaise
- 2 teaspoons crushed red pepper flakes
- 1/4 cup grated Parmesan cheese
- 1/4 cup shredded mozzarella cheese
- 1/4 teaspoon salt
- 1/8 teaspoon ground black pepper

1 Preheat air fryer to 350°F. Spray twelve foil baking liners with cooking spray.

2 Cut puff pastry into twelve even pieces. Place one in each liner.

3 In a large bowl, use a rubber spatula to mix cream cheese, spinach, and mayonnaise until smooth.

4 Add in red pepper flakes, Parmesan, mozzarella, salt, and black pepper and mix until well combined.

5 Place 2 tablespoons mixture into each liner.

6 Place liners into air fryer basket. Bake 7 minutes or until puff pastry is golden brown. Let cool 10 minutes before serving.

PER SERVING

CALORIES: 234 | FAT: 17g | SODIUM: 226mg | CARBOHYDRATES: 15g | FIBER: 1g | SUGAR: 1g | PROTEIN: 4g

Bagel Bombs

These handhelds are a great option for a filling snack. They're not made with premade dough, so you know exactly what's in them. Each bite is a nice little crunch with a creamy inside. For extra flavor, use a flavored cream cheese or sprinkle the tops with everything but the bagel seasoning.

Hands-on time: 15 minutes
Cook time: 12 minutes

Yields 8, 1 per serving

4 ounces cream cheese, frozen
2 cups plus 2 tablespoons bread flour, divided
1 tablespoon baking powder
1/2 teaspoon salt
1 1/2 cups plain full-fat Greek yogurt
1 large egg, whisked

1 Cut cream cheese into 1/2-ounce pieces and roll into balls. Place on a plate and put in the freezer 10 minutes.

2 Preheat air fryer to 320°F.

3 In a large bowl, mix 2 cups flour, baking powder, and salt. Add yogurt and stir until a soft dough forms.

4 Dust a clean work surface with remaining 2 tablespoons flour and turn dough out onto surface. Knead 5 minutes or until dough is smooth and elastic. Shape dough into a disc shape, then cut into eight even pieces.

5 Roll each piece of dough into a ball. Flatten dough out in your hand, then place a piece of cream cheese in the center; form dough around it, pinching the bottom to completely close the seams. Roll between your hands to make a ball.

6 Brush each bagel bite with egg.

7 Place bites into air fryer basket. Bake 12 minutes or until golden brown, flipping when 2 minutes remain for even browning. Serve warm.

PER SERVING

CALORIES: 223 | FAT: 7g | SODIUM: 404mg | CARBOHYDRATES: 28g | FIBER: 1g | SUGAR: 2g | PROTEIN: 9g

Three-Cheese Quiche

You might be surprised to learn that eggs cook well in the air fryer. This café-worthy breakfast is easy to make and just as good as the restaurant version. The soft, cheesy eggs fill every bite with delicious flavor complemented by the buttery pastry dough. Try it with chopped chives on top for a twist.

Hands-on time: 10 minutes
Cook time: 15 minutes

Yields 6, 1 per serving

1 (13.2-ounce) package frozen puff pastry, thawed
6 large eggs
6 tablespoons heavy whipping cream
$2/3$ cup shredded sharp Cheddar cheese
$1/3$ cup shredded Gruyère cheese
$1/4$ cup grated Parmesan cheese
$1/2$ teaspoon salt
$1/4$ teaspoon ground black pepper
2 tablespoons salted butter, melted

CUSTOMIZE IT

The cheeses in this recipe go perfectly with one another and taste great as part of the quiche. If they're not your favorite, however, or not what you have available, you can swap out the cheeses in this recipe for equal parts of another. If you prefer mild Cheddar, Colby, or pepper jack, they are all great options.

1 Preheat air fryer to 320°F. Spray six 4" ramekins with cooking spray.

2 Cut puff pastry into six even pieces. Place a piece into each ramekin, wrapping the top corners slightly over the edge of the ramekin.

3 In a large bowl, whisk together eggs and heavy whipping cream until well combined. Stir in Cheddar, Gruyère, Parmesan, salt, and pepper.

4 Brush a light layer of butter over each piece of puff pastry. Distribute egg mixture evenly among ramekins.

5 Place ramekins into air fryer basket. Bake 15 minutes or until puff pastry is golden brown and top of egg is lightly browned. The egg should feel firm to the touch when done. Serve warm.

PER SERVING

CALORIES: 593 | FAT: 42g | SODIUM: 654mg | CARBOHYDRATES: 30g | FIBER: 1g | SUGAR: 1g | PROTEIN: 17g

Quiche Lorraine

This classic quiche combines a premade pie crust with a cheesy, aromatic filling. This ultra-creamy dish is perfect for special occasions because of the rich flavors. This recipe reheats well for an easy and delicious breakfast too.

Hands-on time: 10 minutes
Cook time: 20 minutes

Serves 8

5 large eggs
1/2 cup heavy whipping cream
1/2 cup shredded Swiss cheese
1/2 cup shredded Gruyère cheese
4 slices bacon, cooked and crumbled
1/3 cup diced yellow onion
3/4 teaspoon salt
1/4 teaspoon ground black pepper
1 (8") premade savory pie crust
1 tablespoon salted butter, melted

1 Preheat air fryer to 320°F.

2 In a large bowl, whisk together eggs and heavy whipping cream.

3 Stir in Swiss, Gruyère, bacon, and onion until well combined. Add salt and pepper and stir to combine.

4 Brush crust with melted butter. Pour in egg mixture and tap gently on the counter to make sure ingredients are in a single even layer.

5 Place into air fryer basket. Bake 20 minutes or until edges are golden brown and the center is firm. Serve warm.

PER SERVING

CALORIES: 319 | FAT: 22g | SODIUM: 546mg | CARBOHYDRATES: 16g | FIBER: 1g | SUGAR: 1g | PROTEIN: 11g

Calzones

Who doesn't love a calzone filled to the brim with delicious toppings? This recipe uses premade dough to make dinner easier than ever. These golden brown Calzones are oozing with cheese. Feel free to add your favorite add-ins such as chopped bell peppers or cooked crumbled sausage.

Hands-on time: 15 minutes
Cook time: 15 minutes

Yields 4, 1 per serving

- 1 (13.8-ounce) tube premade pizza dough
- 1 cup shredded mozzarella cheese
- 4 tablespoons ricotta
- 20 slices pepperoni
- 2 tablespoons salted butter, melted
- 4 tablespoons grated Parmesan cheese
- 1 teaspoon Italian seasoning blend

1 Preheat air fryer to 350°F.

2 Unroll pizza dough and separate into four even sections.

3 Place $1/4$ cup mozzarella and 1 tablespoon ricotta on the bottom half of each piece of dough. Place 5 slices pepperoni on top of each piece.

4 Fold the top half of the dough over the fillings and press the edges together to seal closed.

5 Brush each calzone with butter on each side and sprinkle with Parmesan and Italian seasoning.

6 Place into air fryer basket. Bake 15 minutes, flipping when 5 minutes remain. When done, calzone should be golden brown on both sides. Serve warm.

PER SERVING

CALORIES: 453 | FAT: 19g | SODIUM: 1,042mg | CARBOHYDRATES: 50g | FIBER: 2g | SUGAR: 7g | PROTEIN: 18g

Baked Brie

Brie is soft cheese that turns ultra-creamy when it melts. This recipe makes it the star of any charcuterie board. It's covered in flaky pastry dough that is also great for dipping. It has a buttery flavor that when mixed with a hint of fruit makes the perfect sweet and savory bite.

Hands-on time: 10 minutes
Cook time: 20 minutes

Serves 8

1 (13.2-ounce) package frozen puff pastry, thawed
8-ounce round Brie cheese
$1/4$ cup raspberry preserves
1 large egg
1 tablespoon water

SERVING IDEAS

This recipe is perfect to bring to a dinner party. Place the baked Brie on a large serving platter to catch excess cheese drips. Serve it with seeded crackers and fresh-cut fruit like apples and grapes for a delicious platter that's sure to impress.

1 Preheat air fryer to 375°F.

2 Unroll puff pastry into a rectangle and place Brie in the center. Carefully slice the top $1/2"$ rind off Brie.

3 Spread preserves on top of Brie.

4 Fold puff pastry toward the center of Brie, overlapping slightly and trimming excess dough as needed.

5 In a small bowl, whisk together egg and water. Brush mixture over the entire pastry-wrapped Brie.

6 Place into air fryer basket. Bake 20 minutes or until puff pastry is golden brown. Let cool 10 minutes before serving.

PER SERVING

CALORIES: 388 | **FAT:** 25g | **SODIUM:** 306mg | **CARBOHYDRATES:** 28g | **FIBER:** 1g | **SUGAR:** 5g | **PROTEIN:** 10g

Spinach and Feta-Stuffed Bread

The dough is simple to make, but you can save even more time by using a premade bread dough, found in your local grocer's refrigerated aisle.

Hands-on time: 20 minutes
Cook time: 25 minutes

Serves 8

2 teaspoons sugar
1¼ teaspoons instant yeast
1⅓ cups hot water, around 110°F
2 cups plus 4 tablespoons bread flour, divided
1 tablespoon olive oil
2 cups shredded mozzarella cheese, divided
1 cup crumbled feta
2 cups baby spinach, chopped
3 tablespoons salted butter, melted
1 teaspoon minced garlic
1 cup shredded mild Cheddar cheese

SPICE IT UP!

Try adding 1 teaspoon crushed red pepper flakes to the dough of this bread if you like a little spice. You can also sprinkle a couple teaspoons of your favorite Italian seasoning blend to the top for even more flavor.

1. In a medium bowl, whisk sugar, yeast, and water and let sit 5 minutes or until yeast is foamy.

2. Place 2 cups flour in a large bowl and pour in yeast mixture. Mix gently until just combined. On a clean work surface dusted with 2 tablespoons flour, knead dough 10 minutes or until smooth and elastic.

3. Grease a large bowl with oil. Place dough in bowl and cover with a kitchen towel or plastic wrap. Let rise in a warm place until doubled in size, about 2 hours.

4. On a clean surface dusted with 2 tablespoons flour, roll dough into an 8" × 6" rectangle.

5. On the horizontal bottom half of the dough, sprinkle 1 cup mozzarella and feta.

6. Place spinach on top of cheeses, then fold dough over to cover cheeses and spinach, pressing the edges firmly together to seal.

7. Loosely cover dough with a kitchen towel and let rise for 15 minutes.

8. Preheat air fryer to 320°F. Cut a piece of parchment to fit air fryer basket.

9. Remove towel and place bread on parchment.

10. In a small bowl, mix melted butter and garlic. Pour over bread evenly. Top with remaining 1 cup mozzarella and Cheddar.

11. Place parchment into air fryer basket. Bake 25 minutes or until bread is golden brown. Slice into 1" pieces. Serve warm.

PER SERVING

CALORIES: 349 | FAT: 17g | SODIUM: 450mg | CARBOHYDRATES: 29g | FIBER: 1g | SUGAR: 2g | PROTEIN: 16g

8

Cheesecakes, Custards, and Other Baked Desserts

There are so many baked desserts that can go from the air fryer to the table in practically no time. The list extends far beyond the regular cakes and pies. This chapter is for when you want to get creative and really experience what's possible. I'll bet you've never thought about cooking a fluffy chocolate soufflé in your air fryer or a mouthwatering flan! Believe it or not, the air fryer is perfect for these recipes.

With recipes from Chocolate Lover's Cheesecake to Crème Brûlée, this chapter features a variety of desserts that will inspire a whole new appreciation for air fryer baking!

Vanilla Cheesecake

There's nothing quite like a fresh cheesecake, and you can make a creamy, delicious one right in your air fryer. There's no water bath needed for this dense and flavorful dessert. Each bite has just the right amount of tang to brighten its richness. Add your favorite fruit on top for a fresh twist!

Hands-on time: 15 minutes
Cook time: 18 minutes

Serves 8

16 ounces cream cheese, softened
½ cup granulated sugar
¼ cup sour cream
1 teaspoon vanilla extract
2 teaspoons lemon juice
2 large eggs, whisked
1 (8") premade graham cracker crust

AIR BUBBLES

Stirring in the eggs gently helps avoid excess air bubbles in the batter, so practice caution when you get to that step. Excess air can cause the cheesecake to brown faster and be less smooth and dense. A spatula or wooden spoon is a good tool for this step.

1 Preheat air fryer to 300°F. Spray an 8" round baking dish with cooking spray.

2 In a large bowl, use an electric hand mixer to beat cream cheese until smooth and no lumps remain, about 4 minutes. Mix in sugar, sour cream, vanilla, and lemon juice. Whip until smooth and shiny.

3 Gently stir in eggs until fully combined. Pour mixture into crust, and place crust into prepared dish. Place dish into air fryer basket. Bake 18 minutes or until edges are set and browned and the center jiggles only slightly when tapped.

4 Let cool 2 hours, then transfer to refrigerator to chill at least 4 hours. Serve chilled.

PER SERVING

CALORIES: 390 | FAT: 24g | SODIUM: 335mg | CARBOHYDRATES: 30g | FIBER: 0g | SUGAR: 19g | PROTEIN: 6g

Chocolate Lover's Cheesecake

This cheesecake truly has it all. It's rich, creamy, and loaded with decadent chocolate flavor. This cheesecake has a silk-like texture that will have you coming back to this simple recipe again and again. You may need to share the recipe!

Hands-on time: 16 minutes
Cook time: 18 minutes

Serves 8

16 ounces cream cheese, softened
¼ cup unsweetened cocoa powder
1 (14-ounce) can sweetened condensed milk
1 teaspoon vanilla extract
1 cup milk chocolate chips
2 teaspoons coconut oil
2 large eggs, whisked
1 (8") premade chocolate sandwich cookie crust

1 Preheat air fryer to 320°F.

2 In a large bowl, beat cream cheese until smooth and creamy, about 3 minutes. Mix in cocoa powder, sweetened condensed milk, and vanilla.

3 In a small microwave-safe bowl, melt chocolate chips and coconut oil in microwave in 20-second intervals, stirring between each cook time, about 1 minute.

4 Pour melted chocolate in cream cheese mixture, stirring until fully combined. Using a wooden spoon, gently stir in eggs.

5 Pour batter in crust.

6 Place cheesecake into air fryer basket. Bake 18 minutes or until sides are browned and the center jiggles only slightly. Let cool 2 hours, then transfer to refrigerator to chill at least 6 hours. Serve chilled.

PER SERVING

CALORIES: 522 | FAT: 30g | SODIUM: 383mg | CARBOHYDRATES: 46g | FIBER: 2g | SUGAR: 38g | PROTEIN: 11g

Cheesecake Cookie Bites

When you need a quick treat, this recipe checks all the boxes. It's easy, crunchy, and creamy all in one! Each bite has a variety of textures and a delectable cookies and cream flavor that everyone will love. These have all the delicious cheesecake goodness without the need for a fork and knife.

Hands-on time: 10 minutes
Cook time: 10 minutes

Yields 8, 1 per serving

12 chocolate sandwich cookies, divided
8 ounces cream cheese, softened
$\frac{1}{2}$ cup granulated sugar
1 tablespoon sour cream
1 teaspoon vanilla extract
1 large egg, whisked

COOKIE TYPE

You can swap the sandwich cookies in this recipe for any kind of cookies you'd like. As long as they fit into the foil baking cups, they will work. Chocolate chip cookies would be an excellent swap! And shortbread or sugar cookies would give you the taste of a cheesecake crust.

1 Preheat air fryer to 320°F. Spray eight foil baking liners with cooking spray.

2 Place 1 cookie in each prepared liner. Place remaining 4 cookies in a sealable storage bag and crush into $\frac{1}{4}$" pieces or smaller.

3 In a large bowl, whisk cream cheese and sugar until completely smooth. Stir in sour cream and vanilla until fully combined. Gently stir in egg and fold in crushed cookie pieces.

4 Pour equal amounts batter in liners.

5 Place liners into air fryer basket. Bake 10 minutes or until edges are set and the middles jiggle only slightly.

6 Let cool 30 minutes, then transfer to refrigerator to fully chill, about 2 hours. Serve chilled.

PER SERVING

CALORIES: 242 | FAT: 12g | SODIUM: 182mg | CARBOHYDRATES: 27g | FIBER: 1g | SUGAR: 21g | PROTEIN: 3g

Peanut Butter Cheesecakes

There's a surprising secret to these perfect cheesecakes—don't use too much peanut butter! While it might seem to make sense to pile it up for a ton of flavor, the peanut butter can actually make the cheesecake an undesirable texture. For this recipe, a little goes a long way.

Hands-on time: 11 minutes
Cook time: 12 minutes

Yields 4, 1 per serving

8 ounces cream cheese, softened
1/4 cup creamy peanut butter
2 tablespoons sour cream
1/3 cup granulated sugar
1/2 tablespoon all-purpose flour
1/2 teaspoon vanilla extract
1 large egg, beaten
4 (4") prepared graham cracker crusts
1/4 cup semisweet chocolate chips
1 tablespoon heavy whipping cream

1 Preheat air fryer to 300°F.

2 In a large bowl, whisk together cream cheese, peanut butter, sour cream, and sugar until well combined and smooth.

3 Stir in flour and vanilla until well combined. Stir in egg until just combined. Pour equal amounts batter into crusts.

4 Place cheesecakes into air fryer basket. Bake 12 minutes or until cheesecakes are set and jiggle only slightly in the center. Let cool at least 45 minutes, then refrigerate 2 hours or until completely chilled.

5 In a small microwave-safe bowl, microwave chocolate chips and heavy whipping cream 30 seconds, then stir. The chocolate will be thick but smooth. Drizzle mixture over cheesecakes before serving.

PER SERVING

CALORIES: 556 | **FAT:** 36g | **SODIUM:** 408mg | **CARBOHYDRATES:** 44g | **FIBER:** 2g | **SUGAR:** 32g | **PROTEIN:** 10g

Lemon Pudding Cheesecake

This traditional cheesecake is loaded with lemon flavor without needing fresh lemons. So if lemons aren't in season, you're not out of luck. This recipe uses simple ingredients to make a rich and creamy dessert. Try topping with a spoonful of whipped cream.

Hands-on time: 15 minutes
Cook time: 25 minutes

Serves 6

1 (2.3-ounce) package instant lemon pudding
8 ounces cream cheese, softened
1/4 cup sour cream
1/2 cup granulated sugar
2 large eggs, whisked
1 (8") prepared graham cracker crust

1   Preheat air fryer to 300°F.

2   In a large bowl, mix pudding, cream cheese, sour cream, and sugar until smooth, about 3 minutes.

3   Gently fold in eggs until fully combined. Pour mixture in crust.

4   Place cheesecake into air fryer basket. Bake 25 minutes or until edges are set and the center jiggles only slightly.

5   Let cool 1 hour, then transfer to refrigerator to cool 4 hours or until completely chilled. Serve chilled.

PER SERVING

CALORIES: 427 | FAT: 21g | SODIUM: 364mg | CARBOHYDRATES: 48g | FIBER: 1g | SUGAR: 24g | PROTEIN: 6g

Crème Brûlée

Traditionally, a blowtorch is used to caramelize the sugar on top, but this recipe utilizes the air fryer's concentrated heat to caramelize the top into a lovely golden brown.

Hands-on time: 10 minutes
Cook time: 30 minutes

Serves 2

$1/2$ cup heavy whipping cream
2 tablespoons granulated sugar
1 teaspoon vanilla extract
1 large egg yolk

1 Preheat air fryer to 300°F. Spray two 4" ramekins with cooking spray.

2 In a medium bowl, whisk together all ingredients, then distribute mixture evenly between prepared ramekins.

3 Place ramekins into air fryer basket. Bake 30 minutes or until tops are golden brown. Let cool 30 minutes, then transfer to the refrigerator to cool at least 2 hours. Serve chilled.

PER SERVING

CALORIES: 286 | **FAT:** 23g | **SODIUM:** 26mg | **CARBOHYDRATES:** 15g | **FIBER:** 0g | **SUGAR:** 14g | **PROTEIN:** 3g

Baked Custard

The velvety custard is rich and creamy, with a vanilla flavor and a hint of nutmeg on top to add comfort and spice to every bite. Although it's simple, it's anything but ordinary.

Hands-on time: 5 minutes
Cook time: 20 minutes

Yields 4, 1 per serving

2 cups whole milk
2 large eggs
1 large egg yolk
$1/3$ cup granulated sugar
2 teaspoons vanilla extract
$1/4$ teaspoon ground nutmeg
1 cup whipped cream

1 Preheat air fryer to 320°F. Spray four 4" ramekins with cooking spray.

2 In a large bowl, whisk together all ingredients until well combined. Pour equal amounts mixture in prepared ramekins.

3 Fill an 8" × 8" baking pan with 1" water and place ramekins in water.

4 Place dish with ramekins into air fryer basket. Bake 20 minutes or until custards are firm at edges and jiggle only slightly at the center. Let cool 30 minutes, then chill at least 4 hours. Serve topped with whipped cream.

PER SERVING

CALORIES: 233 | **FAT:** 10g | **SODIUM:** 90mg | **CARBOHYDRATES:** 25g | **FIBER:** 0g | **SUGAR:** 24g | **PROTEIN:** 8g

Flan

Flan is an egg-based custard that is traditionally topped with a caramel sauce. This easy air fryer version cuts the cook time of this creamy and delectable dessert by more than half! Try topping yours with a fresh strawberry for a complementary fruit flavor.

Hands-on time: 10 minutes
Cook time: 35 minutes

Yields 4, 1 per serving

- ½ cup sweetened condensed milk
- ¼ cup plus 2 tablespoons evaporated milk
- 3 large egg yolks
- 4 ounces cream cheese, softened
- 1 teaspoon vanilla extract
- 1 cup granulated sugar

1 Preheat air fryer to 200°F. Spray four 4" ramekins with cooking spray.

2 In a medium bowl, whisk together sweetened condensed milk, evaporated milk, egg yolks, cream cheese, and vanilla until smooth and fully incorporated.

3 In a small saucepan over high heat, add sugar and stir constantly until it begins to clump, about 3 minutes. Continue stirring until it turns into a caramelized liquid, about 2 additional minutes. Pour ¼ cup in each prepared ramekin.

4 Pour equal amounts cream cheese mixture, about ⅓ cup, on top of liquid in each ramekin.

5 Place ramekins into air fryer basket. Bake 30 minutes or until edges and tops are set and the centers jiggle only slightly. Let cool 30 minutes, then chill in refrigerator at least 1 hour until completely chilled.

6 To serve, place a 6" plate upside down on top of each ramekin and flip upside down. The flan should come out cleanly onto the plate and have a golden brown sauce on top.

PER SERVING

CALORIES: 488 | FAT: 16g | SODIUM: 183mg | CARBOHYDRATES: 75g | FIBER: 0g | SUGAR: 72g | PROTEIN: 8g

Raspberry White Chocolate Cheesecake

Cheesecake and fruit go amazingly well together. This cream cheese filling sits on a delectable chocolate cookie crust. The white chocolate adds a richness, and the fruit swirl makes each bite burst with fresh flavor. Feel free to swap the raspberry for your favorite fruit preserves.

Hands-on time: 15 minutes
Cook time: 25 minutes

Serves 8

8 ounces cream cheese, softened
½ cup granulated sugar
⅓ cup white chocolate chips, melted
1 teaspoon lemon juice
½ teaspoon vanilla extract
½ teaspoon cornstarch
1 large egg, beaten
1 (8") premade chocolate cookie pie crust
¼ cup raspberry preserves

1 Preheat air fryer to 300°F.

2 In a large bowl, beat cream cheese and sugar until well combined and completely smooth. Mix in melted white chocolate chips until smooth.

3 Add in lemon juice, vanilla, and cornstarch and stir to combine. Stir in egg until fully combined.

4 Pour mixture in crust. Place small spoonfuls of raspberry preserves in nine separate spots, then use a fork to swirl into cheesecake batter.

5 Place cheesecake into air fryer basket. Bake 25 minutes or until edges are set and the center jiggles only slightly when moved. Let cool 2 hours, then refrigerate and chill at least 4 hours before serving.

PER SERVING

CALORIES: 300 | FAT: 15g | SODIUM: 209mg | CARBOHYDRATES: 34g | FIBER: 0g | SUGAR: 26g | PROTEIN: 3g

Chocolate Soufflés

Chocolate Soufflé is a rich and delicate dessert that is guaranteed to impress. Be sure to serve immediately because, as with traditional soufflés, this dessert will begin to lose its lift and collapse the longer it cools.

Hands-on time: 6 minutes
Cook time: 9 minutes

Yields 2, 1 per serving

1/2 cup milk chocolate chips
1 tablespoon refined coconut oil
2 large eggs, separated, divided

WHIPPING EGG WHITES

To make sure your egg whites will whip properly, make sure none of the yolk remains when you separate the eggs. Be sure the whisk or hand mixer and the bowl are completely dry because even a little bit of water can prevent the egg whites from whipping properly.

1 Preheat air fryer to 350°F. Spray two 4" ramekins with cooking spray.

2 Place chocolate chips and oil in a small microwave-safe bowl. Microwave 30 seconds, then stir and microwave 15 more seconds or until fully melted, about 1 minute. Allow to cool 3 minutes.

3 In a large bowl, use an electric hand mixer on high speed to whip egg whites until stiff peaks form, about 3 minutes.

4 Stir egg yolks into chocolate mixture, then gently fold chocolate mixture into egg whites until fully combined. Distribute evenly between prepared ramekins.

5 Place ramekins into air fryer basket. Bake 9 minutes, then let cool 5 minutes before serving.

PER SERVING

CALORIES: 354 | FAT: 22g | SODIUM: 104mg | CARBOHYDRATES: 25g | FIBER: 1g | SUGAR: 22g | PROTEIN: 9g

Lemon Soufflés

This recipe puts a delightful citrus spin on its chocolaty relative. Though it's a fluffy dessert, it is filled to the brim with rich flavor. Top the finished soufflés with confectioners' sugar before serving to enhance presentation and sweetness.

Hands-on time: 10 minutes
Cook time: 9 minutes

Yields 4, 1 per serving

1 cup white chocolate chips
1 tablespoon salted butter
4 large eggs, separated, divided
¼ teaspoon cream of tartar
2 tablespoons lemon zest

1 Preheat air fryer to 350°F. Spray four 4" ramekins with cooking spray.

2 Place white chocolate chips and butter in a small microwave-safe bowl. Microwave for 30 seconds, then stir and microwave 15 more seconds or until fully melted. Allow to cool 3 minutes.

3 In a large bowl, use an electric hand mixer on high speed to whip egg whites and cream of tartar until stiff peaks form, about 3 minutes.

4 Stir egg yolks and lemon zest into white chocolate mixture, then gently fold white chocolate mixture into egg whites until fully combined. Distribute evenly among prepared ramekins.

5 Place ramekins into air fryer basket. Bake 9 minutes, then let cool 5 minutes before serving.

PER SERVING

CALORIES: 327 | **FAT:** 20g | **SODIUM:** 132mg | **CARBOHYDRATES:** 26g | **FIBER:** 0g | **SUGAR:** 25g | **PROTEIN:** 9g

Pavlova

A Pavlova is a meringue-based dessert with a crunchy exterior and a fluffy, marshmallow-like inside. This recipe is for a base Pavlova, and it can be dressed up in an endless variety of ways for a different flavor profile every time you make it. It's often eaten with fresh fruit.

Hands-on time: 10 minutes
Cook time: 15 minutes

Serves 6

4 large egg whites
1 cup granulated sugar
1/2 teaspoon cream of tartar
2 teaspoons cornstarch

WHIPPING EGG WHITES

To get the fluffiest egg whites, be very careful when separating the yolks. Even the smallest bit of yolk can cause a less fluffy whipped egg white. Another overlooked issue may be the presence of water. Be sure that the bowl and mixer are both completely dry before beginning. Finally, avoid using plastic bowls. They can contain traces of leftover food or grease, whereas glass and aluminum bowls will have a completely clean surface.

1 Preheat air fryer to 200°F. Cut a piece of parchment to fit air fryer basket.

2 In a large bowl, use an electric hand mixer to beat egg whites until soft peaks form, about 3 minutes.

3 In a medium bowl, whisk together sugar, cream of tartar, and cornstarch. Slowly add mixture to egg whites, continuing to beat until stiff peaks form, about 2 minutes.

4 Place mixture on parchment and smooth into an 8" round, 1" thick.

5 Place parchment into air fryer basket. Bake 15 minutes or until firm. Let cool 20 minutes before serving.

PER SERVING

CALORIES: 144 | **FAT:** 0g | **SODIUM:** 36mg | **CARBOHYDRATES:** 34g | **FIBER:** 0g | **SUGAR:** 33g | **PROTEIN:** 2g

Bread Pudding

There's no better use for leftover bread than making delicious bread pudding. This simple dessert uses pantry staples, so you can whip up the creamy classic in no time. Feel free to add chopped nuts or raisins. Just be sure to soak the raisins in water for 10 minutes before mixing them in so they don't burn during baking.

Hands-on time: 10 minutes
Cook time: 25 minutes

Serves 6

2 large eggs
1 cup heavy whipping cream
¼ cup granulated sugar
¼ cup light brown sugar, packed
1 teaspoon vanilla extract
1 teaspoon ground cinnamon
4 tablespoons salted butter, melted
3 cups Italian bread, cut into 1" cubes

1 Preheat air fryer to 350°F. Spray a 6" round baking pan with cooking spray.

2 In a medium bowl, whisk together eggs, heavy whipping cream, granulated sugar, brown sugar, vanilla, cinnamon, and butter until well combined.

3 Place half of the bread in prepared pan, then pour half of the wet mixture over it. Repeat with remaining bread and wet ingredients.

4 Place pan into air fryer basket. Bake 25 minutes or until edges are set and top is golden brown. Let cool for 10 minutes before slicing. Serve warm.

PER SERVING

CALORIES: 345 | FAT: 23g | SODIUM: 209mg | CARBOHYDRATES: 28g | FIBER: 1g | SUGAR: 19g | PROTEIN: 5g

Cinnamon Roll–Baked Oatmeal

This flavorful oatmeal is perfect for cinnamon lovers. And it's a filling breakfast that will keep you full until lunch because of the oats' whole-grain benefits, featuring a big swirl of flavor that will make you feel satisfied.

Hands-on time: 10 minutes
Cook time: 20 minutes

Serves 4

2 cups rolled oats
2 cups whole milk
4 tablespoons salted butter, melted, divided
3 teaspoons ground cinnamon, divided
³/₄ cup light brown sugar, packed, divided
1 teaspoon vanilla extract
1 large egg

1 Preheat air fryer to 320°F. Spray a 6" round baking pan with cooking spray.

2 In a large bowl, stir together oats, milk, 2 tablespoons butter, 2 teaspoons cinnamon, ¹/₂ cup brown sugar, and vanilla. Let sit 5 minutes.

3 Stir in egg until well combined. Pour mixture into prepared pan.

4 Place pan into air fryer basket. Bake 20 minutes or until top is golden brown and firm to the touch. Let cool 10 minutes.

5 To prepare the cinnamon swirl on top, in a small bowl, mix remaining 2 tablespoons butter, 1 teaspoon cinnamon, and ¹/₄ cup brown sugar. Place mixture into a medium storage bag and snip off the end to make a piping bag. Make a swirl over the top of the baked oatmeal. Serve warm.

PER SERVING

CALORIES: 508 | FAT: 18g | SODIUM: 172mg | CARBOHYDRATES: 75g | FIBER: 5g | SUGAR: 47g | PROTEIN: 11g

Maple Walnut–Baked Apples

This recipe is ideal in autumn. Fall flavors like maple and cinnamon come together perfectly to transform simple apples into a sophisticated dessert with the perfect crunch.

Hands-on time: 10 minutes
Cook time: 15 minutes

Yields 8, 1 per serving

- 4 medium Honeycrisp apples
- 1/2 cup chopped walnuts
- 1 teaspoon ground cinnamon
- 1/2 cup quick oats
- 2 tablespoons maple syrup
- 1/4 cup light brown sugar, packed
- 2 tablespoons salted butter, softened

CUSTOMIZE IT

You can get creative with this one to keep it interesting. Feel free to replace the nuts in this recipe with your favorite kind. You can remove them altogether, but you may miss the crunch. You can also top it with cinnamon-sprinkled Greek yogurt or ice cream for a tasty twist.

1 Preheat air fryer to 320°F. Cut a piece of foil to fit air fryer basket.

2 Cut apples in half. Remove the core and seeds and scoop out a 2" hole in the center.

3 Place walnuts and cinnamon into a food processor and pulse five times or until walnuts are finely chopped. Scoop mixture into a medium bowl. Add oats, maple syrup, brown sugar, and butter and mix.

4 Scoop 2 tablespoons mixture into each apple half, pressing down to pack in tightly.

5 Place foil into air fryer basket and place apple halves on top, making sure all the foil corners are weighed down with apples to prevent movement from the air fryer fan. Bake 15 minutes or until apples are tender and oat mixture is golden brown. Let cool 10 minutes, then serve warm.

PER SERVING

CALORIES: 181 | **FAT:** 8g | **SODIUM:** 26mg | **CARBOHYDRATES:** 27g | **FIBER:** 3g | **SUGAR:** 19g | **PROTEIN:** 2g

Brown Sugar Churros

This recipe brings all the yummy flavor from Mexican restaurants right to your kitchen. Churros are usually deep-fried, but with this recipe you can still get a crunchy bite without all the oil. The air fryer makes this sweetened dough golden brown and perfect for dipping in chocolate or caramel sauce.

Hands-on time: 10 minutes
Cook time: 12 minutes

Yields 12, 1 per serving

1 cup whole milk
¼ cup salted butter, cubed
2 tablespoons light brown sugar, packed
1 cup all-purpose flour
1 large egg
1 teaspoon vanilla extract
2 tablespoons granulated sugar
2 teaspoons ground cinnamon

1 Pour milk into a medium saucepan over medium heat. Add butter and whisk in brown sugar. Bring mixture to a boil, about 3 minutes.

2 Add flour, stirring quickly until a smooth dough forms, about 1 minute.

3 Remove from heat and transfer dough to a large bowl. Let cool 5 minutes.

4 Once cooled, mix in egg and vanilla.

5 Preheat air fryer to 350°F. Cut two pieces of parchment to fit air fryer basket.

6 Fill a pastry bag fitted with a rounded star tip with dough. Make twelve 4"-long churros on parchment, using kitchen scissors to cut each churro.

7 Place parchment into air fryer basket, working in batches as needed. Bake 8 minutes or until golden brown, flipping when 2 minutes of cook time remain.

8 In a medium bowl, whisk together granulated sugar and cinnamon. Roll each churro in mixture as soon as it comes out of air fryer. Set aside to cool 5 minutes, then serve immediately.

PER SERVING

CALORIES: 110 | FAT: 5g | SODIUM: 45mg | CARBOHYDRATES: 14g | FIBER: 1g | SUGAR: 5g | PROTEIN: 2g

Dutch Baby

A Dutch Baby, also known as a German pancake, is a light dessert with a crisp, buttery outside and a sweet and fluffy interior. It tastes great topped with everything from confectioners' sugar to fresh fruit to maple syrup!

Hands-on time: 5 minutes
Cook time: 10 minutes

Serves 4

2 tablespoons salted butter, melted
2 large eggs
2 large egg yolks
$^1/_2$ cup all-purpose flour
$^1/_2$ cup buttermilk
2 tablespoons granulated sugar
1 teaspoon vanilla extract
$^1/_4$ teaspoon salt

1 Preheat air fryer to 350°F. Spray a 6" round baking pan with cooking spray.

2 In a large bowl, whisk together all ingredients until well combined. Pour into prepared pan.

3 Place pan into air fryer basket. Bake 10 minutes or until golden brown and firm in the center. When baking, it will puff up but will settle as it cools. Serve warm.

PER SERVING

CALORIES: 216 | FAT: 11g | SODIUM: 262mg | CARBOHYDRATES: 20g | FIBER: 0g | SUGAR: 8g | PROTEIN: 7g

Sweet Potato Fritters

These sweet and crispy fritters are the perfect complement to your holiday meals. A little something different, these taste great as an appetizer or even just a sweet handheld treat.

Hands-on time: 10 minutes
Cook time: 12 minutes

Yields 10, 2 per serving

$^1/_2$ cup cooked mashed sweet potatoes
$^1/_2$ cup mascarpone
$^1/_3$ cup light brown sugar, packed
$^1/_4$ cup self-rising flour

1 Preheat air fryer to 375°F. Cut a piece of parchment to fit air fryer basket.

2 In a large bowl, mix all ingredients together until a soft dough forms.

3 Take heaping tablespoons of dough and place onto parchment. Spray with cooking spray.

4 Place parchment into air fryer basket, working in batches as needed. Bake 12 minutes, flipping after 10 minutes. When done, the fritters will be golden brown at the edges. Let cool for 5 minutes. Serve warm.

PER SERVING

CALORIES: 170 | FAT: 6g | SODIUM: 99mg | CARBOHYDRATES: 27g | FIBER: 1g | SUGAR: 17g | PROTEIN: 3g

Banana Bread Pudding

Fruit lovers will go bananas for this delicious spin on bread pudding. This recipe combines the traditional leftover bread and custard-like filling with warm spices that give this dessert a comforting feel. Enjoy with a scoop of ice cream for even more delectable creaminess.

Hands-on time: 15 minutes
Cook time: 20 minutes

Serves 6

- 2 cups day-old French bread, cut into 1" cubes
- 3/4 cup whole milk
- 1/4 cup heavy whipping cream
- 2 large eggs
- 1/4 cup granulated sugar
- 2 tablespoons light brown sugar, packed
- 2 tablespoons salted butter, melted
- 1/2 teaspoon ground cinnamon
- 1/4 teaspoon ground nutmeg
- 1/4 teaspoon salt
- 1 cup 1/4"-thick banana slices

1 Preheat air fryer to 320°F. Spray an 8" × 8" baking dish with cooking spray.

2 Place bread into prepared dish.

3 In a large bowl, whisk together milk, heavy whipping cream, eggs, granulated sugar, brown sugar, butter, cinnamon, nutmeg, and salt until well combined.

4 Place banana slices on top of bread cubes, then pour the wet mixture over bread and bananas.

5 Place into air fryer basket. Bake 20 minutes or until golden brown and firm. Serve warm.

PER SERVING

CALORIES: 219 | FAT: 10g | SODIUM: 249mg | CARBOHYDRATES: 28g | FIBER: 1g | SUGAR: 18g | PROTEIN: 5g

BANANA BREAD

For an extra dose of banana, you can also use banana bread in place of the French bread. It's an easy way to add extra flavor to this already yummy dish, and it's a perfect way to put that extra banana bread to use so it doesn't go to waste.

Cherry Clafouti

Clafouti is a light French dessert with fresh fruit baked right into its custardy base. The dish is similar to a baked pancake, but has a more elegant flair. Cherries are the traditional fruit used to make clafouti, but you can get as creative as you'd like with raspberries, blueberries, or even peaches.

Hands-on time: 10 minutes
Cook time: 10 minutes

Serves 4

4 large eggs
2 large egg yolks
½ cup granulated sugar
1 cup whole milk
1 teaspoon almond extract
½ teaspoon vanilla extract
½ cup cake flour
¼ teaspoon salt
½ cup halved pitted cherries
2 tablespoons confectioners' sugar

CAKE FLOUR

Cake flour makes this dish extra light. Cake flour contains cornstarch and is finely ground, which helps make things tender. If you don't have any on hand, you can make your own at home in a pinch. Simply mix 7 tablespoons of all-purpose flour and 1 tablespoon of cornstarch together to substitute in this recipe.

1 Preheat air fryer to 320°F. Spray two 6" round baking pans with cooking spray.

2 In a large bowl, whisk eggs and egg yolks until well combined and foamy, about 2 minutes.

3 Add granulated sugar, milk, almond extract, and vanilla, whisking until well combined and foamy at the top.

4 Mix in cake flour and salt until well combined. Pour mixture evenly between prepared pans. Scatter ¼ cup cherry halves over the top of each pan.

5 Place pans into air fryer basket, working in batches as needed. Bake 10 minutes. When done, the top will be very puffy and browned. A minute after the cooking has stopped, the top will deflate but should feel firm to the touch in the center.

6 Sprinkle confectioners' sugar over the top before serving.

PER SERVING

CALORIES: 326 | FAT: 8g | SODIUM: 246mg | CARBOHYDRATES: 49g | FIBER: 1g | SUGAR: 35g | PROTEIN: 11g

Quick Fried Dough

This carnival-inspired recipe is incredibly easy and delicious! The air fryer makes the dough extra crunchy and delicious without having to be deep-fried like traditional fried dough. Feel free to add some chopped fresh berries and a scoop of ice cream to the top to make this perfect summer-style dish.

Hands-on time: 10 minutes
Cook time: 10 minutes

Yields 16, 4 per serving

- 8 ounces frozen bread dough, thawed
- 1 large egg, whisked
- 2 tablespoons salted butter, melted
- $1/2$ cup granulated sugar
- 2 teaspoons ground cinnamon

1 Preheat air fryer to 375°F.

2 Cut bread dough into sixteen even pieces, then flatten into $1/4$"-thick slices.

3 Brush both sides of each slice with egg.

4 Place slices into air fryer basket, working in batches as needed. Bake 10 minutes, flipping for even cooking when 2 minutes remain. The dough will be golden brown when done.

5 Brush each piece of dough with butter.

6 Place sugar and cinnamon in a large storage bag and toss butter-covered dough pieces to fully coat. Let cool for 5 minutes. Serve warm.

PER SERVING

CALORIES: 307 | FAT: 8g | SODIUM: 394mg | CARBOHYDRATES: 53g | FIBER: 2g | SUGAR: 29g | PROTEIN: 6g

Caramel-Baked Pears

Roasting pears in your air fryer is the quickest way to caramelize them and bring out their natural sweetness. This recipe works best with firm Bosc pears, but other varieties of pears will work too. Serve with whipped cream or a scoop of vanilla ice cream for the perfect creamy complement to this rich and fruity dish.

Hands-on time: 5 minutes
Cook time: 6 minutes

Yields 8, 1 per serving

- 4 Bosc pears, halved and cored
- 2 teaspoons lemon juice
- 3 tablespoons light brown sugar, packed
- $\frac{1}{2}$ teaspoon ground cinnamon
- $\frac{1}{2}$ teaspoon pumpkin pie spice
- 3 tablespoons heavy whipping cream

1 Preheat air fryer to 350°F. Spray a 6" round baking pan with cooking spray.

2 Sprinkle pears with lemon juice.

3 Place brown sugar in prepared pan. Sprinkle cinnamon and pumpkin pie spice over brown sugar.

4 Place pears in pan, cut side down. Pour heavy whipping cream over pears.

5 Place pan into air fryer basket. Bake 4 minutes, then turn pears, using a spoon to carefully baste pears with the sauce in pan. Cook an additional 2 minutes or until pears are tender and sauce is bubbling and golden brown. Serve warm.

PER SERVING

CALORIES: 99 | **FAT:** 2g | **SODIUM:** 4mg | **CARBOHYDRATES:** 20g | **FIBER:** 3g | **SUGAR:** 14g | **PROTEIN:** 0g

Mini Baklava Bites

This light and flaky dessert dates back to the Ottoman Empire. Its nutty crunch paired with its delectable sweetness is pure bite-sized bliss. This spiced dessert is perfect for brunch.

Hands-on time: 15 minutes
Cook time: 9 minutes

Yields 15, 3 per serving

- $1/4$ cup granulated sugar
- $1/3$ cup water
- 3 tablespoons honey
- $1/2$ teaspoon lemon juice
- $3/4$ teaspoon ground cinnamon, divided
- $1/4$ teaspoon ground cloves
- 1 cup shelled walnuts
- 1 tablespoon salted butter, softened
- 15 mini phyllo dough shells

1 Place sugar, water, honey, and lemon juice in a small saucepan over medium-high heat. Stir to combine, then continue heating and occasionally stirring. Stir in $1/4$ teaspoon cinnamon and cloves.

2 The mixture should turn a golden brown and begin to thicken after about 5 minutes. Remove from heat.

3 Place walnuts and remaining $1/2$ teaspoon cinnamon into a food processor. Process on high 5 seconds. Add butter and pulse three times or until walnuts are finely chopped and butter is fully incorporated.

4 Place $1/2$ tablespoon walnut mixture into each phyllo shell, gently pressing down to pack in.

5 Place shells into air fryer basket, working in batches as needed. Bake 4 minutes or until shells are golden brown and walnuts begin to turn slightly brown.

6 Carefully remove shells from air fryer basket and place on a work surface. Pour 1 teaspoon cooled syrup in each filled shell. Let soak in 2 minutes, then repeat with an additional teaspoon syrup. Let baklava set at room temperature at least 1 hour before serving.

PER SERVING

CALORIES: 297 | **FAT:** 18g | **SODIUM:** 57mg | **CARBOHYDRATES:** 30g | **FIBER:** 2g | **SUGAR:** 21g | **PROTEIN:** 5g

US/Metric Conversion Chart

VOLUME CONVERSIONS

US Volume Measure	Metric Equivalent
⅛ teaspoon	0.5 milliliter
¼ teaspoon	1 milliliter
½ teaspoon	2 milliliters
1 teaspoon	5 milliliters
½ tablespoon	7 milliliters
1 tablespoon (3 teaspoons)	15 milliliters
2 tablespoons (1 fluid ounce)	30 milliliters
¼ cup (4 tablespoons)	60 milliliters
⅓ cup	90 milliliters
½ cup (4 fluid ounces)	125 milliliters
⅔ cup	160 milliliters
¾ cup (6 fluid ounces)	180 milliliters
1 cup (16 tablespoons)	250 milliliters
1 pint (2 cups)	500 milliliters
1 quart (4 cups)	1 liter (about)

WEIGHT CONVERSIONS

US Weight Measure	Metric Equivalent
½ ounce	15 grams
1 ounce	30 grams
2 ounces	60 grams
3 ounces	85 grams
¼ pound (4 ounces)	115 grams
½ pound (8 ounces)	225 grams
¾ pound (12 ounces)	340 grams
1 pound (16 ounces)	454 grams

OVEN TEMPERATURE CONVERSIONS

Degrees Fahrenheit	Degrees Celsius
200 degrees F	95 degrees C
250 degrees F	120 degrees C
275 degrees F	135 degrees C
300 degrees F	150 degrees C
325 degrees F	160 degrees C
350 degrees F	180 degrees C
375 degrees F	190 degrees C
400 degrees F	205 degrees C
425 degrees F	220 degrees C
450 degrees F	230 degrees C

BAKING PAN SIZES

American	Metric
8 x 1½ inch round baking pan	20 x 4 cm cake tin
9 x 1½ inch round baking pan	23 x 3.5 cm cake tin
11 x 7 x 1½ inch baking pan	28 x 18 x 4 cm baking tin
13 x 9 x 2 inch baking pan	30 x 20 x 5 cm baking tin
2 quart rectangular baking dish	30 x 20 x 3 cm baking tin
15 x 10 x 2 inch baking pan	30 x 25 x 2 cm baking tin (Swiss roll tin)
9 inch pie plate	22 x 4 or 23 x 4 cm pie plate
7 or 8 inch springform pan	18 or 20 cm springform or loose bottom cake tin
9 x 5 x 3 inch loaf pan	23 x 13 x 7 cm or 2 lb narrow loaf or pate tin
1½ quart casserole	1.5 liter casserole
2 quart casserole	2 liter casserole

Index

Note: Page numbers in **bold** indicate recipe category lists.

Quick, easy, & delicious recipes, using 5 INGREDIENTS or less!

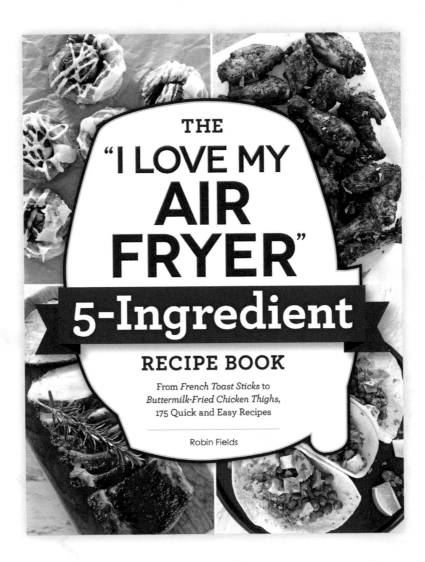

THE
"I LOVE MY
AIR
FRYER"
5-Ingredient
RECIPE BOOK

From *French Toast Sticks* to
Buttermilk-Fried Chicken Thighs,
175 Quick and Easy Recipes

Robin Fields

PICK UP OR DOWNLOAD YOUR COPY TODAY!

adamsmedia
An Imprint of Simon & Schuster
A Paramount Company